# The Power That Raised Jesus from the Dead Is the Corporation behind Our Authority

# The Power That Raised Jesus from the Dead Is the Corporation behind Our Authority

*Compiled by* Eugene Carvalho

*To the Body of Christ.*
*May this compilation bless you richly!*
*With love…*

# TABLE OF CONTENTS

# PURPOSE AND ACKNOWLEDGEMENTS

The infallible Word of God for faith and conduct informs us that the Holy Spirit gives gifts to men and women of the Body of Christ. It states: "the gifts edify the body for the building up of the saints" (Eph. 4:12). I hope the talents and gifts the Lord has given me will be a blessing to someone else through the reading of this compilation.

I am grateful for the love from all family members, especially my wife Mercedes Carvalho. I am also grateful for the knowledge, wisdom and love of many pastors, teachers, and saints that the Lord has used to bless me.

# THE POWER THAT RAISED JESUS FROM THE DEAD

The New Testament warfare book is the book of Ephesians. In it, Paul says, "That the God of our Lord Jesus Christ, the Father of glory, may give unto you the spirit of wisdom and revelation in the knowledge of him: the eyes of your understanding being enlightened; that ye may know what is the hope of his calling, and what the riches of the glory of his inheritance in the saints, and what is the exceeding greatness of his power to us-ward who believe, according to the working of his mighty power" (Eph. 1:17-21 KJV).

These are very powerful verses. "Did you notice this phrase in Ephesians 1:19, "*...the exceeding greatness of his power to usward who believe...?*"

"All the demonstration of the glory of God shown in the manifestation of His omnipotence pointed to man — "to usward."

"The cross of Christ — with what it revealed of obedience to God, atonement for sin, and crushing defeat for the enemies of divine authority — shows us a representative Man.

"Christ was our Representative, our Substitute — overcoming for mankind and preparing a throne and a heavenly ministry for those who should overcome through Him.

"The source of our authority is therefore found in the resurrection and seating of Christ by God. In the book of Ephesians, we learn that God wants the Church to gain revelation knowledge of all that this means to us."[1]

The book of Ephesians is very powerful. I suggest you read the first three chapters in the morning and the last three chapters at night. Do that for a month or two. In these last days, whoever has revelation knowledge will rule the Earth.

Paul informs us in chapter two, "But God, who is rich in mercy, for his great love wherewith he loved us, even when we were dead in sins, hath quickened us together with Christ, (by grace ye are saved;) and hath raised us up together, and made us sit together in heavenly places in Christ Jesus: that in the ages to come he might shew the exceeding riches of his grace in his kindness toward us through Christ Jesus" (Eph. 2:4-7 KJV).

My confession is this, "God has quickened me with Christ. God has raised me up together with Him. God has made me sit together with Christ in heavenly places. As I go about in the earth, working with God in carrying out His plan, I am seated, as far as authority goes, at the Father's right hand."

With that being said, let's examine a vast array of New Testament scriptures that discuss power, Jesus, and authority. They will give you fresh revelation and insight, build your faith, renew your mind, and be a tremendous blessing to you.

---

[1] Kenneth E. Hagin, *Faith Food*, p. 30

# POWER IN THE NEW TESTAMENT

## IN THE BOOK OF MATTHEW

### The Kingdom and the Power and the Glory Forever

"Pray, then, in this way: 'Our Father who is in heaven, Hallowed be Your name. Your kingdom come. Your will be done, On earth as it is in heaven. Give us this day our daily bread. And forgive us our debts, as we also have forgiven our debtors. And do not lead us into temptation, but deliver us from evil. For Yours is the kingdom and the power and the glory forever. Amen.' For if you forgive others for their transgressions, your heavenly Father will also forgive you. But if you do not forgive others, then your Father will not forgive your transgressions" (Mt. 6:9-15).[2]

### Not Understanding the Scriptures nor the Power of God

"But Jesus answered and said to them, 'You are mistaken, not understanding the Scriptures nor the power of God. For in the resurrection they neither marry nor are given in marriage, but are like angels in heaven. But regarding the resurrection of the dead, have you not read what was spoken to you by God: "I AM THE GOD OF ABRAHAM, AND THE GOD OF ISAAC, AND THE GOD OF JACOB"?

---

[2] All Scripture quotations, unless otherwise noted, are from the *New American Standard Bible.*

He is not the God of the dead but of the living.' When the crowds heard this, they were astonished at His teaching" (Mt. 22:29-33).

## With Power and Great Glory

"But immediately after the tribulation of those days THE SUN WILL BE DARKENED, AND THE MOON WILL NOT GIVE ITS LIGHT, AND THE STARS WILL FALL from the sky, and the powers of the heavens will be shaken. And then the sign of the Son of Man will appear in the sky, and then all the tribes of the earth will mourn, and they will see the SON OF MAN COMING ON THE CLOUDS OF THE SKY with power and great glory. And He will send forth His angels with A GREAT TRUMPET and THEY WILL GATHER TOGETHER His elect from the four winds, from one end of the sky to the other" (Mt. 24:29-31).

## At the Right Hand of Power

"Now the chief priests and the whole Council kept trying to obtain false testimony against Jesus, so that they might put Him to death. They did not find any, even though many false witnesses came forward. But later on two came forward, and said, 'This man stated, "I am able to destroy the temple of God and to rebuild it in three days."' The high priest stood up and said to Him, 'Do You not answer? What is it that these men are testifying against You?' But Jesus kept silent. And the high priest said to Him, "I adjure You by the living God, that You tell us whether You are the Christ, the Son of God.' Jesus said to him, 'You have said it yourself; nevertheless I tell you, hereafter you will see THE SON OF MAN SITTING AT THE RIGHT HAND OF POWER, and COMING ON THE CLOUDS OF HEAVEN'" (Mt. 26:59-64).

## IN THE BOOK OF MARK

### The Power Proceeding from Him Had Gone Forth

"A woman who had had a hemorrhage for twelve years, and had endured much at the hands of many physicians, and had spent all that she had and was not helped at all, but rather had grown worse—after hearing about Jesus, she came up in the crowd behind Him and touched His cloak. For she thought, 'If I just touch His garments, I will get well.' Immediately the flow of her blood was dried up; and she felt in her body that she was healed of her affliction. Immediately Jesus, perceiving in Himself that the power proceeding from Him had gone forth, turned around in the crowd and said, 'Who touched My garments?' And His disciples said to Him, 'You see the crowd pressing in on You, and You say, "Who touched Me?"' And He looked around to see the woman who had done this. But the woman fearing and trembling, aware of what had happened to her, came and fell down before Him and told Him the whole truth. And He said to her, 'Daughter, your faith has made you well; go in peace and be healed of your affliction'" (Mk. 5:25-34).

## The Kingdom of God After It Has Come with Power

"And Jesus was saying to them, 'Truly I say to you, there are some of those who are standing here who will not taste death until they see the kingdom of God after it has come with power'" (Mk. 9:1).

### The Scriptures or the Power of God

"Some Sadducees (who say that there is no resurrection) came to Jesus, and began questioning Him, saying, 'Teacher, Moses wrote for us that IF A MAN'S BROTHER DIES and leaves behind a wife AND LEAVES NO CHILD, HIS BROTHER SHOULD MARRY THE WIFE AND RAISE UP CHILDREN TO HIS BROTHER. There were seven brothers; and the first took a wife, and died leaving no children. The second one married her, and died leaving behind no children; and the third likewise; and so all seven left no children. Last of all the woman died also. In the resurrection, when they rise again, which one's wife will she be? For all seven had married her.' Jesus said to them, 'Is this not the reason you are mistaken, that you do not understand the Scriptures or the power of God? For when they rise from the dead, they neither marry nor are given in marriage, but are like angels in heaven. But regarding the fact that the dead rise again, have you not read in the book of Moses, in the passage about the burning bush, how God spoke to him, saying, "I AM THE GOD OF ABRAHAM, AND THE GOD OF ISAAC, and the God of Jacob"? He is not the God of the dead, but of the living; you are greatly mistaken'" (Mk. 12:18-27).

## Coming in Clouds with Great Power and Glory

"But in those days, after that tribulation, THE SUN WILL BE DARKENED AND THE MOON WILL NOT GIVE ITS LIGHT, AND THE STARS WILL BE FALLING from heaven, and the powers that are in the heavens will be shaken. Then they will see THE SON OF MAN COMING IN CLOUDS with great power and glory. And then He will send forth the angels, and will gather together His elect from the four winds, from the farthest end of the earth to the farthest end of heaven" (Mk. 13:24-27).

## Power, and Coming with the Clouds

"They led Jesus away to the high priest; and all the chief priests and the elders and the scribes gathered together. Peter had followed Him at a distance, right into the courtyard of the high priest; and he was sitting with the officers and warming himself at the fire. Now the chief priests and the whole Council kept trying to obtain testimony against Jesus to put Him to death, and they were not finding any. For many were giving false testimony against Him, but their testimony was not consistent. Some stood up and began to give false testimony against Him, saying, 'We heard Him say, "I will destroy this temple made with hands, and in three days I will build another made without hands."' Not even in this respect was their testimony consistent. The high priest stood up and came forward and questioned Jesus, saying, 'Do You not answer? What is it that these men are testifying against You?' But He kept silent and did not answer. Again the high priest was questioning Him, and saying to Him, 'Are You the Christ, the Son of the Blessed One?' And Jesus said, 'I am; and you shall see THE SON OF MAN SITTING AT THE RIGHT HAND OF POWER, and COMING WITH THE CLOUDS OF HEAVEN.' Tearing his clothes, the high priest said, 'What further need do we have of witnesses? You have heard the blasphemy; how does it seem to you?' And they all condemned Him to be deserving of death. Some began to spit at Him, and to blindfold Him, and to beat Him with their fists, and to say to Him, 'Prophesy!' And the officers received Him with slaps in the face" (Mk. 14:53-65).

## IN THE BOOK OF LUKE

### The Power of the Most High Will Overshadow You

"Now in the sixth month the angel Gabriel was sent from God to a city in Galilee called Nazareth, to a virgin engaged to a man whose name was Joseph, of the descendants of David; and the virgin's name was Mary.  And coming in, he said to her, 'Greetings, favored one! The Lord is with you.' But she was very perplexed at this statement, and kept pondering what kind of salutation this was. The angel said to her, 'Do not be afraid, Mary; for you have found favor with God. And behold, you will conceive in your womb and bear a son, and you shall name Him Jesus. He will be great and will be called the Son of the Most High; and the Lord God will give Him the throne of His father David; and He will reign over the house of Jacob forever, and His kingdom will have no end.' Mary said to the angel, 'How can this be, since I am a virgin?' The angel answered and said to her, 'The Holy Spirit will come upon you, and the power of the Most High will overshadow you; and for that reason the holy Child shall be called the Son of God. And behold, even your relative Elizabeth has also conceived a son in her old age; and she who was called barren is now in her sixth month. For nothing will be impossible with God.' And Mary said, 'Behold, the bondslave of the Lord; may it be done to me according to your word.' And the angel departed from her" (Lk. 1:26-38).

## In the Power of the Spirit, and News Spread

"And Jesus returned to Galilee in the power of the Spirit, and news about Him spread through all the surrounding district. And He began teaching in their synagogues and was praised by all" (Lk. 4:14-15).

## For with Authority and Power He Commands

"And He came down to Capernaum, a city of Galilee, and He was teaching them on the Sabbath; and they were amazed at His teaching, for His message was with authority. In the synagogue there was a man possessed by the spirit of an unclean demon, and he cried out with a loud voice, 'Let us alone! What business do we have with each other, Jesus of Nazareth? Have You come to destroy us? I know who You are—the Holy One of God!' But Jesus rebuked him, saying, 'Be quiet and come out of him!' And when the demon had thrown him down in the midst of the people, he came out of him without doing him any harm. And amazement came upon them all, and they began talking with one another saying, 'What is this message? For with authority and power He commands the unclean spirits and they come out.' And the report about Him was spreading into every locality in the surrounding district" (Lk. 4:31-37).

## The Power of the Lord Was Present

"One day He was teaching; and there were some Pharisees and teachers of the law sitting there, who had come from every village of Galilee and Judea and from Jerusalem; and the power of the Lord was present for Him to perform healing. And some men were carrying on a bed a man who was paralyzed; and they were trying to bring him in and to set him down in front of Him. But not finding any way to bring him in because of the crowd, they went up on the roof and let him down through the tiles with his stretcher, into the middle of the crowd, in front of Jesus. Seeing their faith, He said, 'Friend, your sins are forgiven you.' The scribes and the Pharisees began to reason, saying, 'Who is this man who speaks blasphemies? Who can forgive sins, but God alone?' But Jesus, aware of their reasonings, answered and said to them, 'Why are you reasoning in your hearts? Which is easier, to say, "Your sins have been forgiven you," or to say, "Get up and walk"? But, so that you may know that the Son of

Man has authority on earth to forgive sins,'—He said to the paralytic—'I say to you, get up, and pick up your stretcher and go home.' Immediately he got up before them, and picked up what he had been lying on, and went home glorifying God. They were all struck with astonishment and began glorifying God; and they were filled with fear, saying, 'We have seen remarkable things today'" (Lk. 5:17-26).

## Power Was Coming from Him and Healing them All

"Jesus came down with them and stood on a level place; and there was a large crowd of His disciples, and a great throng of people from all Judea and Jerusalem and the coastal region of Tyre and Sidon, who had come to hear Him and to be healed of their diseases; and those who were troubled with unclean spirits were being cured. And all the people were trying to touch Him, for power was coming from Him and healing them all" (Lk. 6:17-19).

## I Was Aware that Power Had Gone Out of Me

"And a woman who had a hemorrhage for twelve years, and could not be healed by anyone, came up behind Him and touched the fringe of His cloak, and immediately her hemorrhage stopped. And Jesus said, 'Who is the one who touched Me?' And while they were all denying it, Peter said, 'Master, the people are crowding and pressing in on You.' But Jesus said, 'Someone did touch Me, for I was aware that power had gone out of Me.' When the woman saw that she had not escaped notice, she came trembling and fell down before Him, and declared in the presence of all the people the reason why she had touched Him, and how she had been immediately healed. And He said to her, 'Daughter, your faith has made you well; go in peace'" (Lk. 8:43-48).

## Power and Authority Over All the Demons

"And He called the twelve together, and gave them power and authority over all the demons and to heal diseases. And He sent them out to proclaim the kingdom of God and to perform healing. And He said to them, 'Take nothing for your journey, neither a staff, nor a bag, nor bread, nor money; and do not even have two tunics apiece. Whatever house you enter, stay there until you leave that city. And as for those who do not receive you, as you go out from that city, shake the dust off your feet as a testimony against them.' Departing, they began going throughout the villages, preaching the gospel and healing everywhere" (Lk. 9:1-6).

## Over All the Power of the Enemy

"The seventy returned with joy, saying, 'Lord, even the demons are subject to us in Your name.' And He said to them, 'I was watching Satan fall from heaven like lightning. Behold, I have given you authority to tread on serpents and scorpions, and over all the power of the enemy, and nothing will injure you. Nevertheless do not rejoice in this, that the spirits are subject to you, but rejoice that your names are recorded in heaven'" (Lk. 10:17-20).

*Chapter Two*

## On a Cloud with Power and Great Glory

"There will be signs in sun and moon and stars, and on the earth dismay among nations, in perplexity at the roaring of the sea and the waves, men fainting from fear and the expectation of the things which are coming upon the world; for the powers of the heavens will be shaken. Then they will see THE SON OF MAN COMING IN A CLOUD with power and great glory. But when these things begin to take place, straighten up and lift up your heads, because your redemption is drawing near" (Lk. 21:25-28).

## At the Right Hand of the Power of God

"When it was day, the Council of elders of the people assembled, both chief priests and scribes, and they led Him away to their council chamber, saying, 'If You are the Christ, tell us.' But He said to them, 'If I tell you, you will not believe; and if I ask a question, you will not answer. But from now on THE SON OF MAN WILL BE SEATED AT THE RIGHT HAND of the power OF GOD.' And they all said, 'Are You the Son of God, then?' And He said to them, 'Yes, I am.' Then they said, 'What further need do we have of testimony? For we have heard it ourselves from His own mouth'" (Lk. 22:66-71).

## Until You Are Clothed with Power from on High

"Now He said to them, 'These are My words which I spoke to you while I was still with you, that all things which are written about Me in the Law of

Moses and the Prophets and the Psalms must be fulfilled.' Then He opened their minds to understand the Scriptures, and He said to them, 'Thus it is written, that the Christ would suffer and rise again from the dead the third day, and that repentance for forgiveness of sins would be proclaimed in His name to all the nations, beginning from Jerusalem. You are witnesses of these things. And behold, I am sending forth the promise of My Father upon you; but you are to stay in the city until you are clothed with power from on high'" (Lk. 24:44-49).

## IN THE BOOK OF ACTS

## You Will Receive Power When the Holy Spirit Has Come upon You

"So when they had come together, they were asking Him, saying, 'Lord, is it at this time You are restoring the kingdom to Israel?' He said to them, 'It is not for you to know times or epochs which the Father has fixed by His own authority; but you will receive power when the Holy Spirit has come upon you; and you shall be My witnesses both in Jerusalem, and in all Judea and Samaria, and even to the remotest part of the earth.' And after He had said these things, He was lifted up while they were looking on, and a cloud received Him out of their sight. And as they were gazing intently into the sky while He was going, behold, two men in white clothing stood beside them. They also said, 'Men of Galilee, why do you stand looking into the sky? This Jesus, who has been taken up from you into heaven, will come in just the same way as you have watched Him go into heaven'" (Ac. 1:6-11).

## As if by Our Own Power or Piety

"While he was clinging to Peter and John, all the people ran together to them at the so-called portico of Solomon, full of amazement. But when Peter saw this, he replied to the people, 'Men of Israel, why are you amazed at this, or why do you gaze at us, as if by our own power or piety we had made him walk? The God of Abraham, Isaac and Jacob, the God of our fathers, has glorified His servant Jesus, the one whom you delivered and disowned in the presence of Pilate, when he had decided to release Him. But you disowned the Holy and Righteous One and asked for a murderer to be granted to you, but put to death the Prince of life, the one whom God raised from the dead, a fact to which we are witnesses. And on the basis of faith in His name, it is the name of Jesus which has strengthened this man whom you see and know; and the faith which comes through Him has given him this perfect health in the presence of you all'" (Ac. 3:11-16).

## And with Great Power They Were
## Giving Testimony

"And the congregation of those who believed were of one heart and soul; and not one of them claimed that anything belonging to him was his own, but all things were common property to them. And with great power the apostles were giving testimony to the resurrection of the Lord Jesus, and abundant grace was upon them all. For there was not a needy person among them, for all who were owners of land or houses would sell them and bring the proceeds of the sales and lay them at the apostles' feet, and they would be distributed to each as any had need" (Ac. 4:32-35).

## Full of Grace and Power, Was Performing Wonders

"And Stephen, full of grace and power, was performing great wonders and signs among the people. But some men from what was called the Synagogue of the Freedmen, including both Cyrenians and Alexandrians, and some from Cilicia and Asia, rose up and argued with Stephen. But they were unable to cope with the wisdom and the Spirit with which he was speaking. Then they secretly induced men to say, 'We have heard him speak blasphemous words against Moses and against God.' And they stirred up the people, the elders and the scribes, and they came up to him and dragged him away and brought him before the Council. They put forward false witnesses who said, 'This man incessantly speaks against this holy place and the Law; for we have heard him say that this Nazarene, Jesus, will destroy this place and alter the customs which Moses handed down to us.' And fixing their gaze on him, all who were sitting in the Council saw his face like the face of an angel" (Ac. 6:8-15).

*Chapter Two*

# This Man Is What Is Called the Great Power of God

"Now there was a man named Simon, who formerly was practicing magic in the city and astonishing the people of Samaria, claiming to be someone great; and they all, from smallest to greatest, were giving attention to him, saying, 'This man is what is called the Great Power of God.' And they were giving him attention because he had for a long time astonished them with his magic arts. But when they believed Philip preaching the good news about the kingdom of God and the name of Jesus Christ, they were being baptized, men and women alike. Even Simon himself believed; and after being baptized, he continued on with Philip, and as he observed signs and great miracles taking place, he was constantly amazed" (Ac. 8:9-13).

## With the Holy Spirit and with Power

"Opening his mouth, Peter said: 'I most certainly understand now that God is not one to show partiality, but in every nation the man who fears Him and does what is right is welcome to Him. The word which He sent to the sons of Israel, preaching peace through Jesus Christ (He is Lord of all)—you yourselves know the thing which took place throughout all Judea, starting from Galilee, after the baptism which John proclaimed. You know of Jesus of Nazareth, how God anointed Him with the Holy Spirit and with power, and how He went about doing good and healing all who were oppressed by the devil, for God was with Him. We are witnesses of all the things He did both in the land of the Jews and in Jerusalem. They also put Him to death by hanging Him on a cross. God raised Him up on the third day and granted that He become visible,  not to all the people, but to witnesses who were chosen beforehand by God, that is, to us who ate and drank with Him after He arose from the dead. And He ordered us to preach to the people, and solemnly to testify that this is the One who has been appointed by God as Judge of the living and the dead. Of Him all the prophets bear witness that through His name everyone who believes in Him receives forgiveness of sins'" (Ac. 10:34-43).

## IN THE BOOK OF ROMANS

### With Power by the Resurrection from the Dead

"Paul, a bond-servant of Christ Jesus, called as an apostle, set apart for the gospel of God, which He promised beforehand through His prophets in the holy Scriptures, concerning His Son, who was born of a descendant of David according to the flesh, who was declared the Son of God with power by the resurrection from the dead, according to the Spirit of holiness, Jesus Christ our Lord, through whom we have received grace and apostleship to bring about the obedience of faith among all the Gentiles for His name's sake, among whom you also are the called of Jesus Christ; to all who are beloved of God in Rome, called as saints: Grace to you and peace from God our Father and the Lord Jesus Christ" (Ro. 1:1-7).

## It Is the Power of God for Salvation

"For I am not ashamed of the gospel, for it is the power of God for salvation to everyone who believes, to the Jew first and also to the Greek. For in it the righteousness of God is revealed from faith to faith; as it is written, 'BUT THE RIGHTEOUS man SHALL LIVE BY FAITH'" (Ro. 1:16-17).

## His Attributes and Eternal Power Have Been Clearly Seen

"For the wrath of God is revealed from heaven against all ungodliness and unrighteousness of men who suppress the truth in unrighteousness, because that which is known about God is evident within them; for God made it evident to them. For since the creation of the world His invisible attributes, His eternal power and divine nature, have been clearly seen, being understood through what has been made, so that they are without excuse. For even though they knew God, they did not honor Him as God or give thanks, but they became futile in their speculations, and their foolish heart was darkened. Professing to be wise, they became fools, and exchanged the glory of the incorruptible God for an image in the form of corruptible man and of birds and four-footed animals and crawling creatures" (Ro. 1:18-23).

### To Demonstrate My Power in You

"What shall we say then? There is no injustice with God, is there? May it never be! For He says to

Moses, 'I WILL HAVE MERCY ON WHOM I HAVE MERCY, AND I WILL HAVE COMPASSION ON WHOM I HAVE COMPASSION.' So then it does not depend on the man who wills or the man who runs, but on God who has mercy. For the Scripture says to Pharaoh, 'FOR THIS VERY PURPOSE I RAISED YOU UP, TO DEMONSTRATE MY POWER IN YOU, AND THAT MY NAME MIGHT BE PROCLAIMED THROUGHOUT THE WHOLE EARTH.' So then He has mercy on whom He desires, and He hardens whom He desires" (Ro. 9:14-18).

## Demonstrate His Wrath and to Make His Power Known

"You will say to me then, 'Why does He still find fault? For who resists His will?" On the contrary, who are you, O man, who answers back to God? The thing molded will not say to the molder, 'Why did you make me like this," will it? Or does not the potter have a right over the clay, to make from the same lump one vessel for honorable use and another for common use? What if God, although willing to demonstrate His wrath and to make His power known, endured with much patience vessels of wrath prepared for destruction? And He did so to make known the riches of His glory upon vessels of mercy, which He prepared beforehand for glory, even us, whom He also called, not from among Jews only, but also from among Gentiles. As He says also in Hosea, 'I WILL CALL THOSE WHO WERE NOT MY PEOPLE, "MY PEOPLE," AND HER WHO WAS NOT BELOVED, "BELOVED." AND IT

SHALL BE THAT IN THE PLACE WHERE IT WAS SAID TO THEM, "YOU ARE NOT MY PEOPLE," THERE THEY SHALL BE CALLED SONS OF THE LIVING GOD'" (Ro. 9:19-26).

## Abound in Hope by the Power of the Holy Spirit.

"Again Isaiah says, 'THERE SHALL COME THE ROOT OF JESSE, AND HE WHO ARISES TO RULE OVER THE GENTILES, IN HIM SHALL THE GENTILES HOPE.' Now may the God of hope fill you with all joy and peace in believing, so that you will abound in hope by the power of the Holy Spirit" (Ro. 15:12-13).

## The Power of Signs and Wonders

"And concerning you, my brethren, I myself also am convinced that you yourselves are full of goodness, filled with all knowledge and able also to admonish one another. But I have written very boldly to you on some points so as to remind you again, because of the grace that was given me from God, to be a minister of Christ Jesus to the Gentiles, ministering as a priest the gospel of God, so that my offering of the Gentiles may become acceptable, sanctified by the Holy Spirit. Therefore in Christ Jesus I have found reason for boasting in things pertaining to God. For I will not presume to speak of anything except what Christ has accomplished through me, resulting in the obedience of the Gentiles by word and deed, in the power of signs and wonders, in the power of the Spirit; so that from Jerusalem and round about as far as Illyricum I have fully preached the gospel of Christ. And thus I aspired to preach the gospel, not where Christ was already named, so that I would not build on another man's foundation; but as it is written, 'THEY WHO HAD NO NEWS OF HIM SHALL SEE, AND THEY WHO HAVE NOT HEARD SHALL UNDERSTAND'" (Ro. 15:14-21).

## IN THE BOOK OF 1 CORINTHIANS

### Christ the Power of God and the Wisdom of God

"For the word of the cross is foolishness to those who are perishing, but to us who are being saved it is the power of God. For it is written, 'I WILL DESTROY THE WISDOM OF THE WISE, AND THE CLEVERNESS OF THE CLEVER I WILL SET ASIDE.' Where is the wise man? Where is the scribe? Where is the debater of this age? Has not God made foolish the wisdom of the world? For since in the wisdom of God the world through its wisdom did not come to know God, God was well-pleased through the foolishness of the message preached to save those who believe. For indeed Jews ask for signs and Greeks search for wisdom; but we preach Christ crucified, to Jews a stumbling block and to Gentiles foolishness, but to those who are the called, both Jews and Greeks, Christ the power of God and the wisdom of God. Because the foolishness of God is wiser than men, and the weakness of God is stronger than men" (1Co. 1:18-25).

*Chapter Two*

# Preaching in Demonstration of the Spirit and of Power

"And when I came to you, brethren, I did not come with superiority of speech or of wisdom, proclaiming to you the testimony of God. For I determined to know nothing among you except Jesus Christ, and Him crucified. I was with you in weakness and in fear and in much trembling, and my message and my preaching were not in persuasive words of wisdom, but in demonstration of the Spirit and of power, so that your faith would not rest on the wisdom of men, but on the power of God" (1Co. 2:1-5).

## Does Not Consist in Words but in Power

"I do not write these things to shame you, but to admonish you as my beloved children. For if you were to have countless tutors in Christ, yet you would not have many fathers, for in Christ Jesus I became your father through the gospel. Therefore I exhort you, be imitators of me. For this reason I have sent to you Timothy, who is my beloved and faithful child in the Lord, and he will remind you of my ways which are in Christ, just as I teach everywhere in every church. Now some have become arrogant, as though I were not coming to you. But I will come to you soon, if the Lord wills, and I shall find out, not the words of those who are arrogant but their power. For the kingdom of God does not consist in words but in power. What do you desire? Shall I come to you with a rod, or with love and a spirit of gentleness" (1Co. 4:14-21)?

## The Power of Our Lord Jesus

"For I, on my part, though absent in body but present in spirit, have already judged him who has so committed this, as though I were present. In the name of our Lord Jesus, when you are assembled, and I with you in spirit, with the power of our Lord Jesus, I have decided to deliver such a one to Satan for the destruction of his flesh, so that his spirit may be saved in the day of the Lord Jesus" (1Co. 5:3-5).

## Will Also Raise Us up Through His Power

"All things are lawful for me, but not all things are profitable. All things are lawful for me, but I will not be mastered by anything. Food is for the stomach and the stomach is for food, but God will do away with both of them. Yet the body is not for immorality, but for the Lord, and the Lord is for the body. Now God has not only raised the Lord, but will also raise us up through His power. Do you not know that your bodies are members of Christ? Shall I then take away the members of Christ and make them members of a prostitute? May it never be! Or do you not know that the one who joins himself to a prostitute is one body with her? For He says, 'THE TWO SHALL BECOME ONE FLESH.' But the one who joins himself to the Lord is one spirit with Him. Flee immorality. Every other sin that a man commits is outside the body, but the immoral man sins against his own body. Or do you not know that your body is a temple of the Holy Spirit who is in you, whom you have from God, and that you are not your own? For you have been bought with a price:

therefore glorify God in your body" (1Co. 6:12-20).

## He Has Abolished All Rule and All Authority and Power

"But now Christ has been raised from the dead, the first fruits of those who are asleep. For since by a man came death, by a man also came the resurrection of the dead. For as in Adam all die, so also in Christ all will be made alive. But each in his own order: Christ the first fruits, after that those who are Christ's at His coming,  then comes the end, when He hands over the kingdom to the God and Father, when He has abolished all rule and all authority and power. For He must reign until He has put all His enemies under His feet. The last enemy that will be abolished is death. For HE HAS PUT ALL THINGS IN SUBJECTION UNDER HIS FEET. But when He says, 'All things are put in subjection,' it is evident that He is excepted who put all things in subjection to Him. When all things are subjected to Him, then the Son Himself also will be subjected to the One who subjected all things to Him, so that God may be all in all" (1Co. 15:20-28).

## It Is Sown in Weakness, It Is Raised in Power

"So also is the resurrection of the dead. It is sown a perishable body, it is raised an imperishable body; it is sown in dishonor, it is raised in glory; it is sown in weakness, it is raised in power; it is sown a natural body, it is raised a spiritual body. If there is a natural body, there is also a spiritual body. So also it is written, 'The first MAN, Adam, BECAME A

LIVING SOUL.' The last Adam became a life-giving spirit. However, the spiritual is not first, but the natural; then the spiritual. The first man is from the earth, earthy; the second man is from heaven. As is the earthy, so also are those who are earthy; and as is the heavenly, so also are those who are heavenly. Just as we have borne the image of the earthy, we will also bear the image of the heavenly" (1Co. 15:42-49).

## IN THE BOOK OF 2 CORINTHIANS

### The Power Will Be of God

"But we have this treasure in earthen vessels, so that the surpassing greatness of the power will be of God and not from ourselves; we are afflicted in every way, but not crushed; perplexed, but not despairing; persecuted, but not forsaken; struck down, but not destroyed; always carrying about in the body the dying of Jesus, so that the life of Jesus also may be manifested in our body. For we who live are constantly being delivered over to death for Jesus' sake, so that the life of Jesus also may be manifested in our mortal flesh. So death works in us, but life in you" (2Co. 4:7-12).

### The Power of God; by the Weapons
### of Righteousness

"And working together with Him, we also urge you not to receive the grace of God in vain—for He says, 'AT THE ACCEPTABLE TIME I LISTENED TO YOU, AND ON THE DAY OF SALVATION I

HELPED YOU.' Behold, now is 'THE ACCEPTABLE TIME,' behold, now is 'THE DAY OF SALVATION' — giving no cause for offense in anything, so that the ministry will not be discredited, but in everything commending ourselves as servants of God, in much endurance, in afflictions, in hardships, in distresses, in beatings, in imprisonments, in tumults, in labors, in sleeplessness, in hunger, in purity, in knowledge, in patience, in kindness, in the Holy Spirit, in genuine love, in the word of truth, in the power of God; by the weapons of righteousness for the right hand and the left, by glory and dishonor, by evil report and good report; regarded as deceivers and yet true; as unknown yet well-known, as dying yet behold, we live; as punished yet not put to death, as sorrowful yet always rejoicing, as poor yet making many rich, as having nothing yet possessing all things" (2Co. 6:1-10).

## Power Is Perfected in Weakness

"Boasting is necessary, though it is not profitable; but I will go on to visions and revelations of the Lord. I know a man in Christ who fourteen years ago — whether in the body I do not know, or out of the body I do not know, God knows — such a man was caught up to the third heaven. And I know how such a man — whether in the body or apart from the body I do not know, God knows — was caught up into Paradise and heard inexpressible words, which a man is not permitted to speak. On behalf of such a man I will boast; but on my own behalf I will not boast, except in regard to my weaknesses. For if I do wish to boast I will not be foolish, for I will be speaking the truth; but I refrain from this, so that no one will credit me with more than he sees in me or hears from me. Because of the surpassing greatness of the revelations, for this reason, to keep me from exalting myself, there was given me a thorn in the flesh, a messenger of Satan to torment me — to keep me from exalting myself! Concerning this I implored the Lord three times that it might leave me. And He has said to me, 'My grace is sufficient for you, for power is perfected in weakness.' Most gladly, therefore, I will rather boast about my weaknesses, so that the power of Christ may dwell in me. Therefore I am well content with weaknesses, with insults, with distresses, with persecutions, with difficulties, for Christ's sake; for when I am weak, then I am strong" (2Co. 12:1-10).

## He Lives Because of the Power of God

"This is the third time I am coming to you. EVERY FACT IS TO BE CONFIRMED BY THE TESTIMONY OF TWO OR THREE WITNESSES. I have previously said when present the second time, and though now absent I say in advance to those who have sinned in the past and to all the rest as well, that if I come again I will not spare anyone, since you are seeking for proof of the Christ who speaks in me, and who is not weak toward you, but mighty in you. For indeed He was crucified because of weakness, yet He lives because of the power of God. For we also are weak in Him, yet we will live with Him because of the power of God directed toward you" (2Co. 13:1-4).

*Chapter Two*

# IN THE BOOK OF EPHESIANS

## Far Above All Rule and Authority and Power

"For this reason I too, having heard of the faith in the Lord Jesus which exists among you and your love for all the saints, do not cease giving thanks for you, while making mention of you in my prayers; that the God of our Lord Jesus Christ, the Father of glory, may give to you a spirit of wisdom and of revelation in the knowledge of Him. I pray that the eyes of your heart may be enlightened, so that you will know what is the hope of His calling, what are the riches of the glory of His inheritance in the saints, and what is the surpassing greatness of His power toward us who believe. These are in accordance with the working of the strength of His might which He brought about in Christ, when He raised Him from the dead and seated Him at His right hand in the heavenly places, far above all rule and authority and power and dominion, and every name that is named, not only in this age but also in the one to come. And He put all things in subjection under His feet, and gave Him as head over all things to the church, which is His body, the fullness of Him who fills all in all" (Eph. 1:15-23).

## Me According to the Working of His Power

"For this reason I, Paul, the prisoner of Christ Jesus for the sake of you Gentiles—if indeed you have heard of the stewardship of God's grace which was given to me for you; that by revelation there was made known to me the mystery, as I wrote before in brief. By referring to this, when you read you can understand my insight into the mystery of Christ, which in other generations was not made known to the sons of men, as it has now been revealed to His holy apostles and prophets in the Spirit; to be specific, that the Gentiles are fellow heirs and fellow members of the body, and fellow partakers of the promise in Christ Jesus through the gospel, of which I was made a minister, according to the gift of God's grace which was given to me according to the working of His power. To me, the very least of all saints, this grace was given, to preach to the Gentiles the unfathomable riches of Christ, and to bring to light what is the administration of the mystery which for ages has been hidden in God who created all things; so that the manifold wisdom of God might now be made known through the church to the rulers and the authorities in the heavenly places. This was in accordance with the eternal purpose which He carried out in Christ Jesus our Lord, in whom we have boldness and confident access through faith in Him. Therefore I ask you not to lose heart at my tribulations on your behalf, for they are your glory" (Eph. 3:1-13).

## Strengthened with Power Through His Spirit

"For this reason I bow my knees before the Father,  from whom every family in heaven and on earth derives its name, that He would grant you, according to the riches of His glory, to be strengthened with power through His Spirit in the inner man, so that Christ may dwell in your hearts through faith; and that you, being rooted and grounded in love, may be able to comprehend with all the saints what is the breadth and length and height and depth, and to know the love of Christ which surpasses knowledge, that you may be filled up to all the fullness of God" (Eph. 3:14-19).

## According to the Power that Works Within Us

"Now to Him who is able to do far more abundantly beyond all that we ask or think, according to the power that works within us, to Him be the glory in the church and in Christ Jesus to all generations forever and ever. Amen" (Eph. 3:20-21).

## IN THE BOOK OF PHILIPPIANS

### Know Him and the Power of His Resurrection

"But whatever things were gain to me, those things I have counted as loss for the sake of Christ. More than that, I count all things to be loss in view of the surpassing value of knowing Christ Jesus my Lord, for whom I have suffered the loss of all things, and count them but rubbish so that I may gain Christ, and may be found in Him, not having a righteousness of my own derived from the Law, but that which is through faith in Christ, the righteousness which comes from God on the basis of faith, that I may know Him and the power of His resurrection and the fellowship of His sufferings, being conformed to His death; in order that I may attain to the resurrection from the dead" (Php. 3:7-11).

*Chapter Two*

## The Exertion of the Power

"Brethren, join in following my example, and observe those who walk according to the pattern you have in us. For many walk, of whom I often told you, and now tell you even weeping, that they are enemies of the cross of Christ, whose end is destruction, whose god is their appetite, and whose glory is in their shame, who set their minds on earthly things. For our citizenship is in heaven, from which also we eagerly wait for a Savior, the Lord Jesus Christ; who will transform the body of our humble state into conformity with the body of His glory, by the exertion of the power that He has even to subject all things to Himself" (Php. 3:17-21).

## IN THE BOOK OF COLOSSIANS

## Strengthened with All Power

"For this reason also, since the day we heard of it, we have not ceased to pray for you and to ask that you may be filled with the knowledge of His will in all spiritual wisdom and understanding, so that you will walk in a manner worthy of the Lord, to please Him in all respects, bearing fruit in every good work and increasing in the knowledge of God; strengthened with all power, according to His glorious might, for the attaining of all steadfastness and patience; joyously giving thanks to the Father, who has qualified us to share in the inheritance of the saints in Light. For He rescued us from the domain of darkness, and transferred us to the kingdom of His beloved Son, in whom we have redemption, the forgiveness of sins" (Col. 1:9-14).

## His Power, Which Mightily Works Within Me

"Now I rejoice in my sufferings for your sake, and in my flesh I do my share on behalf of His body, which is the church, in filling up what is lacking in Christ's afflictions. Of this church I was made a minister according to the stewardship from God bestowed on me for your benefit, so that I might fully carry out the preaching of the word of God, that is, the mystery which has been hidden from the past ages and generations, but has now been manifested to His saints, to whom God willed to make known what is the riches of the glory of this mystery among the Gentiles, which is Christ in you, the hope of glory. We proclaim Him, admonishing every man and teaching every man with all wisdom, so that we may present every man complete in Christ. For this purpose also I labor, striving according to His power, which mightily works within me" (Col. 1:24-29).

## IN THE BOOK OF 1 THESSALONIANS

## In Power and in the Holy Spirit and with Full Conviction

"We give thanks to God always for all of you, making mention of you in our prayers; constantly bearing in mind your work of faith and labor of love and steadfastness of hope in our Lord Jesus Christ in the presence of our God and Father, knowing, brethren beloved by God, His choice of you; for our gospel did not come to you in word only, but also in power and in the Holy Spirit and with full conviction; just as you know what kind of men we proved to be among you for your sake. You also became imitators of us and of the Lord, having received the word in much tribulation with the joy of the Holy Spirit, so that you became an example to all the believers in Macedonia and in Achaia. For the word of the Lord has sounded forth from you, not only in Macedonia and Achaia, but also in every place your faith toward God has gone forth, so that we have no need to say anything.  For they themselves report about us what kind of a reception we had with you, and how you turned to God from idols to serve a living and true God, and to wait for His Son from heaven, whom He raised from the dead, that is Jesus, who rescues us from the wrath to come" (1Th. 1:2-10).

## IN THE BOOK OF 2 THESSALONIANS

### Away from the Glory of His Power

"We ought always to give thanks to God for you, brethren, as is only fitting, because your faith is greatly enlarged, and the love of each one of you toward one another grows ever greater; therefore, we ourselves speak proudly of you among the churches of God for your perseverance and faith in the midst of all your persecutions and afflictions which you endure. This is a plain indication of God's righteous judgment so that you will be considered worthy of the kingdom of God, for which indeed you are suffering. For after all it is only just for God to repay with affliction those who afflict you, and to give relief to you who are afflicted and to us as well when the Lord Jesus will be revealed from heaven with His mighty angels in flaming fire, dealing out retribution to those who do not know God and to those who do not obey the gospel of our Lord Jesus. These will pay the penalty of eternal destruction, away from the presence of the Lord and from the glory of His power, when He comes to be glorified in His saints on that day, and to be marveled at among all who have believed—for our testimony to you was believed. To this end also we pray for you always, that our God will count you worthy of your calling, and fulfill every desire for goodness and the work of faith with power, so that the name of our Lord Jesus will be glorified in you, and you in Him, according to the grace of our God and the Lord Jesus Christ" (2Th. 1:3-12).

## IN THE BOOK OF 2 TIMOTHY

### But of Power and Love and Discipline

"I thank God, whom I serve with a clear conscience the way my forefathers did, as I constantly remember you in my prayers night and day, longing to see you, even as I recall your tears, so that I may be filled with joy. For I am mindful of the sincere faith within you, which first dwelt in your grandmother Lois and your mother Eunice, and I am sure that it is in you as well. For this reason I remind you to kindle afresh the gift of God which is in you through the laying on of my hands. For God has not given us a spirit of timidity, but of power and love and discipline" (2Ti. 1:3-7).

## Suffering for the Gospel According to the Power of God

"Therefore do not be ashamed of the testimony of our Lord or of me His prisoner, but join with me in suffering for the gospel according to the power of God, who has saved us and called us with a holy calling, not according to our works, but according to His own purpose and grace which was granted us in Christ Jesus from all eternity, but now has been revealed by the appearing of our Savior Christ Jesus, who abolished death and brought life and immortality to light through the gospel, for which I was appointed a preacher and an apostle and a teacher. For this reason I also suffer these things, but I am not ashamed; for I know whom I have believed and I am convinced that He is able to guard what I have entrusted to Him until that day. Retain the standard of sound words which you have heard from me, in the faith and love which are in Christ Jesus. Guard, through the Holy Spirit who dwells in us, the treasure which has been entrusted to you" (2Ti. 1:8-14).

## They Denied Its Power; Avoid Such Men as These

"But realize this, that in the last days difficult times will come. For men will be lovers of self, lovers of money, boastful, arrogant, revilers, disobedient to parents, ungrateful, unholy, unloving, irreconcilable, malicious gossips, without self-control, brutal, haters of good, treacherous, reckless, conceited, lovers of pleasure rather than lovers of God, holding to a form of godliness, although they have denied its power; Avoid such men as these. For among them are those who enter into households and captivate weak women weighed down with sins, led on by various impulses, always learning and never able to come to the knowledge of the truth. Just as Jannes and Jambres opposed Moses, so these men also oppose the truth, men of depraved mind, rejected in regard to the faith. But they will not make further progress; for their folly will be obvious to all, just as Jannes's and Jambres's folly was also" (2Ti. 3:1-9).

## IN THE BOOK OF HEBREWS

### All Things by the Word of His Power

"God, after He spoke long ago to the fathers in the prophets in many portions and in many ways, in these last days has spoken to us in His Son, whom He appointed heir of all things, through whom also He made the world. And He is the radiance of His glory and the exact representation of His nature, and upholds all things by the word of His power. When He had made purification of sins, He sat down at the right hand of the Majesty on high, having become as much better than the angels, as He has inherited a more excellent name than they" (Heb. 1:1-4).

### The Power of Death

"Therefore, since the children share in flesh and blood, He Himself likewise also partook of the same, that through death He might render powerless him who had the power of death, that is, the devil, and might free those who through fear of death were subject to slavery all their lives. For assuredly He does not give help to angels, but He gives help to the descendant of Abraham. Therefore, He had to be made like His brethren in all things, so that He might become a merciful and faithful high priest in things pertaining to God, to make propitiation for the sins of the people. For since He Himself was tempted in that which He has suffered, He is able to come to the aid of those who are tempted" (Heb. 2:14-18).

## IN THE BOOK OF 1 PETER

### Protected by the Power of God Through Faith

"Blessed be the God and Father of our Lord Jesus Christ, who according to His great mercy has caused us to be born again to a living hope through the resurrection of Jesus Christ from the dead, to obtain an inheritance which is imperishable and undefiled and will not fade away, reserved in heaven for you, who are protected by the power of God through faith for a salvation ready to be revealed in the last time. In this you greatly rejoice, even though now for a little while, if necessary, you have been distressed by various trials, so that the proof of your faith, being more precious than gold which is perishable, even though tested by fire, may be found to result in praise and glory and honor at the revelation of Jesus Christ; and though you have not seen Him, you love Him, and though you do not see Him now, but believe in Him, you greatly rejoice with joy inexpressible and full of glory, obtaining as the outcome of your faith the salvation of your souls" (1Pe. 1:3-9).

## IN THE BOOK OF 2 PETER

### His Divine Power Has Granted to Us Everything

"Simon Peter, a bond-servant and apostle of Jesus Christ, To those who have received a faith of the same kind as ours, by the righteousness of our God and Savior, Jesus Christ: Grace and peace be multiplied to you in the knowledge of God and of Jesus our Lord; seeing that His divine power has granted to us everything pertaining to life and godliness, through the true knowledge of Him who called us by His own glory and excellence. For by these He has granted to us His precious and magnificent promises, so that by them you may become partakers of the divine nature, having escaped the corruption that is in the world by lust. Now for this very reason also, applying all diligence, in your faith supply moral excellence, and in your moral excellence, knowledge, and in your knowledge, self-control, and in your self-control, perseverance, and in your perseverance, godliness, and in your godliness, brotherly kindness, and in your brotherly kindness, love. For if these qualities are yours and are increasing, they render you neither useless nor unfruitful in the true knowledge of our Lord Jesus Christ. For he who lacks these qualities is blind or short-sighted, having forgotten his purification from his former sins. Therefore, brethren, be all the more diligent to make certain about His calling and choosing you; for as long as you practice these things, you will never stumble; for in this way the entrance into the eternal kingdom of our Lord and Savior Jesus Christ will be abundantly supplied to you" (2Pe. 1:1-11).

## We Made Known to You the Power

"For we did not follow cleverly devised tales when we made known to you the power and coming of our Lord Jesus Christ, but we were eyewitnesses of His majesty. For when He received honor and glory from God the Father, such an utterance as this was made to Him by the Majestic Glory, "This is My beloved Son with whom I am well-pleased" — and we ourselves heard this utterance made from heaven when we were with Him on the holy mountain" (2Pe. 1:16-18).

## IN THE BOOK OF REVELATION

## Our God, to Receive Glory and Honor and Power

"After these things I looked, and behold, a door standing open in heaven, and the first voice which I had heard, like the sound of a trumpet speaking with me, said, 'Come up here, and I will show you what must take place after these things.' Immediately I was in the Spirit; and behold, a throne was standing in heaven, and One sitting on the throne. And He who was sitting was like a jasper stone and a sardius in appearance; and there was a rainbow around the throne, like an emerald in appearance. Around the throne were twenty-four thrones; and upon the thrones I saw twenty-four elders sitting, clothed in white garments, and golden crowns on their heads. Out from the throne come flashes of lightning and sounds and peals of thunder. And there were seven lamps of fire burning before the throne, which are the seven Spirits of God; and before the throne there was something like a sea of glass, like crystal; and in the center and around the throne, four living creatures full of eyes in front and behind. The first creature was like a lion, and the second creature like a calf, and the third creature had a face like that of a man, and the fourth creature was like a flying eagle. And the four living creatures, each one of them having six wings, are full of eyes around and within; and day and night they do not cease to say, 'HOLY, HOLY, HOLY is THE LORD GOD, THE ALMIGHTY, WHO WAS AND WHO IS AND WHO IS TO COME.' And when the living creatures give glory and honor and thanks to Him who sits on the throne, to Him who lives forever and ever, the twenty-four elders will fall down before Him who sits on the throne, and will worship Him who lives forever and ever, and will cast their crowns before the throne, saying, 'Worthy are You, our Lord and our God, to receive glory and honor and power; for You created all things, and because of Your will they existed, and were created'" (Rev. 4:1-11).

*Chapter Two*

## Worthy Is the Lamb to Receive Power, Riches, Wisdom, Might, Honor, Glory and Blessing

"Then I looked, and I heard the voice of many angels around the throne and the living creatures and the elders; and the number of them was myriads of myriads, and thousands of thousands, saying with a loud voice, 'Worthy is the Lamb that was slain to receive power and riches and wisdom and might and honor and glory and blessing.' And every created thing which is in heaven and on the earth and under the earth and on the sea, and all things in them, I heard saying, 'To Him who sits on the throne, and to the Lamb, be blessing and honor and glory and dominion forever and ever.' And the four living creatures kept saying, 'Amen.' And the elders fell down and worshiped" (Rev. 5:11-14).

## Honor and Power and Might, Be to Our God Forever

"After these things I looked, and behold, a great multitude which no one could count, from every nation and all tribes and peoples and tongues, standing before the throne and before the Lamb, clothed in white robes, and palm branches were in their hands; and they cry out with a loud voice, saying, 'Salvation to our God who sits on the throne, and to the Lamb.' And all the angels were standing around the throne and around the elders and the four living creatures; and they fell on their faces before the throne and worshiped God, saying, 'Amen, blessing and glory and wisdom and thanksgiving and honor and power and might, be to our God forever and ever. Amen'" (Rev. 7:9-12).

## Your Great Reigning Power

"Then the seventh angel sounded; and there were loud voices in heaven, saying, 'The kingdom of the world has become the kingdom of our Lord and of His Christ; and He will reign forever and ever.' And the twenty-four elders, who sit on their thrones before God, fell on their faces and worshiped God, saying, 'We give You thanks, O Lord God, the Almighty, who are and who were, because You have taken Your great power and have begun to reign. And the nations were enraged, and Your wrath came, and the time came for the dead to be judged, and the time to reward Your bond-servants the prophets and the saints and those who fear Your name, the small and the great, and to destroy those who destroy the earth'" (Rev. 11:15-18).

## Salvation, Power, Authority, and Kingdom
## of Christ

"And there was war in heaven, Michael and his angels waging war with the dragon. The dragon and his angels waged war, and they were not strong enough, and there was no longer a place found for them in heaven. And the great dragon was thrown down, the serpent of old who is called the devil and Satan, who deceives the whole world; he was thrown down to the earth, and his angels were thrown down with him. Then I heard a loud voice in heaven, saying, 'Now the salvation, and the power, and the kingdom of our God and the authority of

His Christ have come, for the accuser of our brethren has been thrown down, he who accuses them before our God day and night. And they overcame him because of the blood of the Lamb and because of the word of their testimony, and they did not love their life even when faced with death. For this reason, rejoice, O heavens and you who dwell in them. Woe to the earth and the sea, because the devil has come down to you, having great wrath, knowing that he has only a short time'" (Rev. 12:7-12).

## From the Glory of God and from His Power

"After these things I looked, and the temple of the tabernacle of testimony in heaven was opened, and the seven angels who had the seven plagues came out of the temple, clothed in linen, clean and bright, and girded around their chests with golden sashes. Then one of the four living creatures gave to the seven angels seven golden bowls full of the wrath of God, who lives forever and ever. And the temple was filled with smoke from the glory of God and from His power; and no one was able to enter the temple until the seven plagues of the seven angels were finished" (Rev. 15:5-8).

## God Who Has the Power over These Plagues

"The fourth angel poured out his bowl upon the sun, and it was given to it to scorch men with fire. Men were scorched with fierce heat; and they blasphemed the name of God who has the power over these plagues, and they did not repent so as to give Him glory" (Rev. 16:8-9).

*Chapter Two*

## Hallelujah! Salvation, Glory and Power
## Belong to God

"After these things I heard something like a loud voice of a great multitude in heaven, saying, 'Hallelujah! Salvation and glory and power belong to our God;   BECAUSE HIS JUDGMENTS ARE TRUE AND RIGHTEOUS; for He has judged the great harlot who was corrupting the earth with her immorality, and HE HAS AVENGED THE BLOOD OF HIS BOND-SERVANTS ON HER.' And a second time they said, 'Hallelujah! HER SMOKE RISES UP FOREVER AND EVER.' And the twenty-four elders and the four living creatures fell down and worshiped God who sits on the throne saying, 'Amen. Hallelujah!' And a voice came from the throne, saying, 'Give praise to our God, all you His bond-servants, you who fear Him, the small and the great.' Then I heard something like the voice of a great multitude and like the sound of many waters and like the sound of mighty peals of thunder, saying, 'Hallelujah! For the Lord our God, the Almighty, reigns. Let us rejoice and be glad and give the glory to Him, for the marriage of the Lamb has come and His bride has made herself ready.' It was given to her to clothe herself in fine linen, bright and clean; for the fine linen is the righteous acts of the saints" (Rev. 19:1-8).

*Chapter Three*

# JESUS IN THE EPISTLES

## THE BOOK OF ROMANS

### You Also Are the Called of Jesus Christ

"Paul, a bond-servant of Christ Jesus, called as an apostle, set apart for the gospel of God, which He promised beforehand through His prophets in the holy Scriptures, concerning His Son, who was born of a descendant of David according to the flesh, who was declared the Son of God with power by the resurrection from the dead, according to the Spirit of holiness, Jesus Christ our Lord, through whom we have received grace and apostleship to bring about the obedience of faith among all the Gentiles for His name's sake, among whom you also are the called of Jesus Christ" (Ro. 1:1-6).

### I Thank My God Through Jesus Christ for You All, Because Your Faith

"First, I thank my God through Jesus Christ for you all, because your faith is being proclaimed throughout the whole world. For God, whom I serve in my spirit in the preaching of the gospel of His Son, is my witness as to how unceasingly I make mention of you, always in my prayers making request, if perhaps now at last by the will of God I may succeed in coming to you. For I long to see you so that I may impart some spiritual gift to you, that you may be established; that is, that I may be encouraged together with you while among you, each of us by the other's faith, both yours and mine. I do not want you to be unaware, brethren, that often I have planned to come to you (and have been prevented so far) so that I may obtain some fruit among you also, even as among the rest of the Gentiles. I am under obligation both to Greeks and to barbarians, both to the wise and to the foolish. So, for my part, I am eager to preach the gospel to you also who are in Rome" (Ro. 1:8-15).

## God Will Judge the Secrets of Men through Christ Jesus

"But if you bear the name 'Jew' and rely upon the Law and boast in God, and know His will and approve the things that are essential, being instructed out of the Law, and are confident that you yourself are a guide to the blind, a light to those who are in darkness, a corrector of the foolish, a teacher of the immature, having in the Law the embodiment of knowledge and of the truth, you, therefore, who teach another, do you not teach yourself? You who preach that one shall not steal, do you steal? You who say that one should not commit adultery, do you commit adultery? You who abhor idols, do you rob temples? You who boast in the Law, through your breaking the Law, do you dishonor God? For 'THE NAME OF GOD IS BLASPHEMED AMONG THE GENTILES BECAUSE OF YOU,' just as it is written" (Ro. 2:17-24).

# The Righteousness of God Through Faith in Jesus Christ for All Those Who Believe

"But now apart from the Law the righteousness of God has been manifested, being witnessed by the Law and the Prophets, even the righteousness of God through faith in Jesus Christ for all those who believe; for there is no distinction; for all have sinned and fall short of the glory of God, being justified as a gift by His grace through the redemption which is in Christ Jesus; whom God displayed publicly as a propitiation in His blood through faith. This was to demonstrate His righteousness, because in the forbearance of God He passed over the sins previously committed; for the demonstration, I say, of His righteousness at the present time, so that He would be just and the justifier of the one who has faith in Jesus" (Ro. 3:21-26).

## Those Who Believe in Him Who Raised Jesus Our Lord from the Dead

"For this reason it is by faith, in order that it may be in accordance with grace, so that the promise will be guaranteed to all the descendants, not only to those who are of the Law, but also to those who are of the faith of Abraham, who is the father of us all, (as it is written, 'A FATHER OF MANY NATIONS HAVE I MADE YOU') in the presence of Him whom he believed, even God, who gives life to the dead and calls into being that which does not exist. In hope against hope he believed, so that he might become a father of many nations according to that which had been spoken, 'SO SHALL YOUR DESCENDANTS BE.' Without becoming weak in faith he contemplated his own body, now as good as dead since he was about a hundred years old, and the deadness of Sarah's womb; yet, with respect to the promise of God, he did not waver in unbelief but grew strong in faith, giving glory to God, and being fully assured that what God had promised, He was able also to perform. Therefore IT WAS ALSO CREDITED TO HIM AS RIGHTEOUSNESS. Now not for his sake only was it written that it was credited to him, but for our sake also, to whom it will be credited, as those who believe in Him who raised Jesus our Lord from the dead, He who was delivered over because of our transgressions, and was raised because of our justification" (Ro. 4:16-25).

## We Have Peace with God Through Our Lord Jesus

"Therefore, having been justified by faith, we have peace with God through our Lord Jesus Christ, through whom also we have obtained our introduction by faith into this grace in which we stand; and we exult in hope of the glory of God. And not only this, but we also exult in our tribulations, knowing that tribulation brings about perseverance; and perseverance, proven character; and proven character, hope; and hope does not disappoint, because the love of God has been poured out within our hearts through the Holy Spirit who was given to us" (Ro. 5:1-5).

# We Also Exult in God Through Our Lord Jesus Christ

"Therefore, just as through one man sin entered into the world, and death through sin, and so death spread to all men, because all sinned—for until the Law sin was in the world, but sin is not imputed when there is no law. Nevertheless death reigned from Adam until Moses, even over those who had not sinned in the likeness of the offense of Adam, who is a type of Him who was to come" (Ro. 5:12-14).

## Will Reign in Life through the One, Jesus Christ

"But the free gift is not like the transgression. For if by the transgression of the one the many died, much more did the grace of God and the gift by the grace of the one Man, Jesus Christ, abound to the many. The gift is not like that which came through the one who sinned; for on the one hand the judgment arose from one transgression resulting in condemnation, but on the other hand the free gift arose from many transgressions resulting in justification. For if by the transgression of the one, death reigned through the one, much more those who receive the abundance of grace and of the gift of righteousness will reign in life through the One, Jesus Christ" (Ro. 5:15-17).

## To Eternal Life Through Jesus Christ Our Lord

"So then as through one transgression there resulted condemnation to all men, even so through one act of righteousness there resulted justification of life to all men. For as through the one man's disobedience the many were made sinners, even so through the obedience of the One the many will be made righteous. The Law came in so that the transgression would increase; but where sin increased, grace abounded all the more, so that, as sin reigned in death, even so grace would reign through righteousness to eternal life through Jesus Christ our Lord" (Ro. 5:18-21).

## All of Us Who Have Been Baptized into Christ Jesus Have Been Baptized into His Death

"What shall we say then? Are we to continue in sin so that grace may increase? May it never be! How shall we who died to sin still live in it? Or do you not know that all of us who have been baptized into Christ Jesus have been baptized into His death? Therefore we have been buried with Him through baptism into death, so that as Christ was raised from the dead through the glory of the Father, so we too might walk in newness of life. For if we have become united with Him in the likeness of His death, certainly we shall also be in the likeness of His resurrection, knowing this, that our old self was crucified with Him, in order that our body of sin might be done away with, so that we would no longer be slaves to sin; for he who has died is freed from sin" (Ro. 6:1-7).

*Chapter Three*

# Consider Yourselves to Be Dead to Sin, but Alive to God in Christ Jesus

"Now if we have died with Christ, we believe that we shall also live with Him, knowing that Christ, having been raised from the dead, is never to die again; death no longer is master over Him. For the death that He died, He died to sin once for all; but the life that He lives, He lives to God. Even so consider yourselves to be dead to sin, but alive to God in Christ Jesus" (Ro. 6:8-11).

## The Free Gift of God Is Eternal Life in Christ Jesus Our Lord

"For when you were slaves of sin, you were free in regard to righteousness. Therefore what benefit were you then deriving from the things of which you are now ashamed? For the outcome of those things is death. But now having been freed from sin and enslaved to God, you derive your benefit, resulting in sanctification, and the outcome, eternal life. For the wages of sin is death, but the free gift of God is eternal life in Christ Jesus our Lord" (Ro. 6:20-23).

## There Is Therefore Now No Condemnation for Those Who Are in Christ Jesus

"Therefore there is now no condemnation for those who are in Christ Jesus. For the law of the Spirit of life in Christ Jesus has set you free from the law of sin and of death. For what the Law could not do, weak as it was through the flesh, God did:

sending His own Son in the likeness of sinful flesh and as an offering for sin, He condemned sin in the flesh, so that the requirement of the Law might be fulfilled in us, who do not walk according to the flesh but according to the Spirit. For those who are according to the flesh set their minds on the things of the flesh, but those who are according to the Spirit, the things of the Spirit. For the mind set on the flesh is death, but the mind set on the Spirit is life and peace, because the mind set on the flesh is hostile toward God; for it does not subject itself to the law of God, for it is not even able to do so, and those who are in the flesh cannot please God" (Ro. 8:1-8).

## He Who Raised Christ Jesus from the Dead Will Also Give Life to Your Mortal Bodies

"However, you are not in the flesh but in the Spirit, if indeed the Spirit of God dwells in you. But if anyone does not have the Spirit of Christ, he does not belong to Him. If Christ is in you, though the body is dead because of sin, yet the spirit is alive because of righteousness. But if the Spirit of Him who raised Jesus from the dead dwells in you, He who raised Christ Jesus from the dead will also give life to your mortal bodies through His Spirit who dwells in you" (Ro. 8:9-11).

## Nothing Shall Separate Us from the Love of God, Which Is in Christ Jesus Our Lord

"What then shall we say to these things? If God is for us, who is against us? He who did not spare His own Son, but delivered Him over for us all, how will He not also with Him freely give us all things? Who will bring a charge against God's elect? God is the one who justifies; who is the one who condemns? Christ Jesus is He who died, yes, rather who was raised, who is at the right hand of God, who also intercedes for us. Who will separate us from the love of Christ? Will tribulation, or distress, or persecution, or famine, or nakedness, or peril, or sword? Just as it is written, 'FOR YOUR SAKE WE ARE BEING PUT TO DEATH ALL DAY LONG; WE WERE CONSIDERED AS SHEEP TO BE SLAUGHTERED.' But in all these things we overwhelmingly conquer through Him who loved us. For I am convinced that neither death, nor life, nor angels, nor principalities, nor things present, nor things to come, nor powers, nor height, nor depth, nor any other created thing, will be able to separate us from the love of God, which is in Christ Jesus our Lord" (Ro. 8:31-39).

## Confess with Your Mouth and Believe in Your Heart that God Raised Him from the Dead, You Shall Be Saved

"For Moses writes that the man who practices the righteousness which is based on law shall live by that righteousness. But the righteousness based on faith speaks as follows: 'DO NOT SAY IN YOUR HEART, "WHO WILL ASCEND INTO HEAVEN?" (that is, to bring Christ down), or "WHO WILL DESCEND INTO THE ABYSS?" (that is, to bring Christ up from the dead).' But what does it say? "THE WORD IS NEAR YOU, in your mouth and in your heart'—that is, the word of faith which we are preaching, that if you confess with your mouth Jesus as Lord, and believe in your heart that God raised Him from the dead, you will be saved; for with the heart a person believes, resulting in righteousness, and with the mouth he confesses, resulting in salvation. For the Scripture says, 'WHOEVER BELIEVES IN HIM WILL NOT BE DISAPPOINTED.' For there is no distinction between Jew and Greek; for the same Lord is Lord of all, abounding in riches for all who call on Him; for 'WHOEVER WILL CALL ON THE NAME OF THE LORD WILL BE SAVED'" (Ro. 10:5-13).

## Put on the Lord Jesus Christ, and Make No Provision for the Flesh

"Do this, knowing the time, that it is already the hour for you to awaken from sleep; for now salvation is nearer to us than when we believed. The night is almost gone, and the day is near. Therefore let us lay aside the deeds of darkness and put on the armor of light. Let us behave properly as in the day, not in carousing and drunkenness, not in sexual promiscuity and sensuality, not in strife and jealousy. But put on the Lord Jesus Christ, and make no provision for the flesh in regard to its lusts" (Ro. 13:11-14).

## In the Lord Jesus

"Therefore let us not judge one another anymore, but rather determine this—not to put an obstacle or a stumbling block in a brother's way. I know and am convinced in the Lord Jesus that nothing is unclean in itself; but to him who thinks anything to be unclean, to him it is unclean. For if because of food your brother is hurt, you are no longer walking according to love. Do not destroy with your food him for whom Christ died. Therefore do not let what is for you a good thing be spoken of as evil; for the kingdom of God is not eating and drinking, but righteousness and peace and joy in the Holy Spirit. For he who in this way serves Christ is acceptable to God and approved by men. So then we pursue the things which make for peace and the building up of one another. Do not tear down the work of God for the sake of food. All things indeed are clean, but they are evil for the man who eats and gives offense. It is good not to eat meat or to drink wine, or to do anything by which your brother stumbles. The faith which you have, have as your own conviction before God. Happy is he who does not condemn himself in what he approves. But he who doubts is condemned if he eats, because his eating is not from faith; and whatever is not from faith is sin" (Ro. 14:13-23).

## Be of the Same Mind with One Another According to Christ Jesus

"Now we who are strong ought to bear the weaknesses of those without strength and not just please ourselves. Each of us is to please his neighbor for his good, to his edification. For even Christ did not please Himself; but as it is written, 'THE REPROACHES OF THOSE WHO REPROACHED YOU FELL ON ME.' For whatever was written in earlier times was written for our instruction, so that through perseverance and the encouragement of the Scriptures we might have hope. Now may the God who gives perseverance and encouragement grant you to be of the same mind with one another according to Christ Jesus, so that with one accord you may with one voice glorify the God and Father of our Lord Jesus Christ" (Ro. 15:1-6).

## To Be a Minister of Christ Jesus to the Gentiles

"And concerning you, my brethren, I myself also am convinced that you yourselves are full of goodness, filled with all knowledge and able also to admonish one another. But I have written very boldly to you on some points so as to remind you again, because of the grace that was given me from God, to be a minister of Christ Jesus to the Gentiles, ministering as a priest the gospel of God, so that my offering of the Gentiles may become acceptable, sanctified by the Holy Spirit. Therefore in Christ Jesus I have found reason for boasting in things pertaining to God. For I will not presume to speak of anything except what Christ has accomplished through me, resulting in the obedience of the Gentiles by word and deed, in the power of signs and wonders, in the power of the Spirit; so that from Jerusalem and round about as far as Illyricum I have fully preached the gospel of Christ. And thus I aspired to preach the gospel, not where Christ was already named, so that I would not build on another man's foundation; but as it is written, 'THEY WHO HAD NO NEWS OF HIM SHALL SEE, AND THEY WHO HAVE NOT HEARD SHALL

UNDERSTAND'" (Ro. 15:14-21).

## By Our Lord Jesus Christ and by the Love of the Spirit, to Strive Together with Me

"Now I urge you, brethren, by our Lord Jesus Christ and by the love of the Spirit, to strive together with me in your prayers to God for me, that I may be rescued from those who are disobedient in Judea, and that my service for Jerusalem may prove acceptable to the saints; so that I may come to you in joy by the will of God and find refreshing rest in your company. Now the God of peace be with you all. Amen" (Ro. 15:30-33).

## The Grace of Our Lord Jesus Be with You

"Now I urge you, brethren, keep your eye on those who cause dissensions and hindrances contrary to the teaching which you learned, and turn away from them. For such men are slaves, not of our Lord Christ but of their own appetites; and by their smooth and flattering speech they deceive the hearts of the unsuspecting. For the report of your obedience has reached to all; therefore I am rejoicing over you, but I want you to be wise in what is good and innocent in what is evil. The God of peace will soon crush Satan under your feet. The grace of our Lord Jesus be with you" (Ro. 16:17-20).

*Chapter Three*

## According to My Gospel and the Preaching of Jesus Christ

"Now to Him who is able to establish you according to my gospel and the preaching of Jesus Christ, according to the revelation of the mystery which has been kept secret for long ages past, but now is manifested, and by the Scriptures of the prophets, according to the commandment of the eternal God, has been made known to all the nations, leading to obedience of faith; to the only wise God, through Jesus Christ, be the glory forever. Amen" (Ro. 16:25-27).

## THE BOOK OF 1 CORINTHIANS

## Confirm You to the End, Blameless in the Day of Our Lord Jesus Christ

"I thank my God always concerning you for the grace of God which was given you in Christ Jesus, that in everything you were enriched in Him, in all speech and all knowledge, even as the testimony concerning Christ was confirmed in you, so that you are not lacking in any gift, awaiting eagerly the revelation of our Lord Jesus Christ, who will also confirm you to the end, blameless in the day of our Lord Jesus Christ. God is faithful, through whom you were called into fellowship with His Son, Jesus Christ our Lord" (1Co. 1:4-9).

*Chapter Three*

## Now I Exhort You, Brethren, by the Name of Our Lord Jesus Christ

"Now I exhort you, brethren, by the name of our Lord Jesus Christ, that you all agree and that there be no divisions among you, but that you be made complete in the same mind and in the same judgment. For I have been informed concerning you, my brethren, by Chloe's people, that there are quarrels among you. Now I mean this, that each one of you is saying, 'I am of Paul,' and 'I of Apollos,' and 'I of Cephas,' and 'I of Christ.' Has Christ been divided? Paul was not crucified for you, was he? Or were you baptized in the name of Paul? I thank God that I baptized none of you except Crispus and Gaius, so that no one would say you were baptized in my name. Now I did baptize also the household of Stephanas; beyond that, I do not know whether I baptized any other. For Christ did not send me to baptize, but to preach the gospel, not in cleverness of speech, so that the cross of Christ would not be made void" (1Co. 1:10-17).

## By His Doing You Are in Christ Jesus

"For consider your calling, brethren, that there were not many wise according to the flesh, not many mighty, not many noble; but God has chosen the foolish things of the world to shame the wise, and God has chosen the weak things of the world to shame the things which are strong, and the base things of the world and the despised God has chosen, the things that are not, so that He may nullify the things that are, so that no man may boast before God. But by His doing you are in Christ Jesus, who became to us wisdom from God, and righteousness and sanctification, and redemption, so that, just as it is written, 'LET HIM WHO BOASTS, BOAST IN THE LORD'" (1Co. 1:26-31).

## For I Determined to Know Nothing Among You Except Jesus Christ, and Him Crucified

"And when I came to you, brethren, I did not come with superiority of speech or of wisdom, proclaiming to you the testimony of God. For I determined to know nothing among you except Jesus Christ, and Him crucified. I was with you in weakness and in fear and in much trembling, and my message and my preaching were not in persuasive words of wisdom, but in demonstration of the Spirit and of power, so that your faith would not rest on the wisdom of men, but on the power of God" (1Co. 2:1-5).

## A Foundation Other than the One Which Is Laid, Which Is Jesus Christ

"According to the grace of God which was given to me, like a wise master builder I laid a foundation, and another is building on it. But each man must be careful how he builds on it. For no man can lay a foundation other than the one which is laid, which is Jesus Christ. Now if any man builds on the foundation with gold, silver, precious stones, wood, hay, straw, each man's work will become evident; for the day will show it because it is to be revealed with fire, and the fire itself will test the quality of each man's work. If any man's work which he has built on it remains, he will receive a reward. If any man's work is burned up, he will suffer loss; but he himself will be saved, yet so as through fire" (1Co. 3:10-15).

## In Christ Jesus I Became Your Father Through the Gospel

"I do not write these things to shame you, but to admonish you as my beloved children. For if you were to have countless tutors in Christ, yet you would not have many fathers, for in Christ Jesus I became your father through the gospel. Therefore I exhort you, be imitators of me. For this reason I have sent to you Timothy, who is my beloved and faithful child in the Lord, and he will remind you of my ways which are in Christ, just as I teach everywhere in every church. Now some have become arrogant, as though I were not coming to you. But I will come to you soon, if the Lord wills, and I shall find out, not the words of those who are arrogant but their power. For the kingdom of God does not consist in words but in power. What do you desire? Shall I come to you with a rod, or with love and a spirit of gentleness" (1Co. 4:14-21)?

## That His Spirit May Be Saved in the Day of the Lord Jesus

"For I, on my part, though absent in body but present in spirit, have already judged him who has so committed this, as though I were present. In the name of our Lord Jesus, when you are assembled, and I with you in spirit, with the power of our Lord Jesus, I have decided to deliver such a one to Satan for the destruction of his flesh, so that his spirit may be saved in the day of the Lord Jesus" (1Co. 5:3-5).

## In the Name of the Lord Jesus Christ, and in the Spirit of Our God

"Or do you not know that the unrighteous will not inherit the kingdom of God? Do not be deceived; neither fornicators, nor idolaters, nor adulterers, nor effeminate, nor homosexuals, nor thieves, nor the covetous, nor drunkards, nor revilers, nor swindlers, will inherit the kingdom of God. Such were some of you; but you were washed, but you were sanctified, but you were justified in the name of the Lord Jesus Christ and in the Spirit of our God" (1Co. 6:9-11).

## One Lord, Jesus Christ, by Whom Are All Things, and We Exist Through Him

"Therefore concerning the eating of things sacrificed to idols, we know that there is no such thing as an idol in the world, and that there is no God but one. For even if there are so-called gods whether in heaven or on earth, as indeed there are many gods and many lords, yet for us there is but one God, the Father, from whom are all things and we exist for Him; and one Lord, Jesus Christ, by whom are all things, and we exist through Him" (1Co. 8:4-6).

*Chapter Three*

## The Lord Jesus in the Night in Which He Was Betrayed Took Bread

"For I received from the Lord that which I also delivered to you, that the Lord Jesus in the night in which He was betrayed took bread; and when He had given thanks, He broke it and said, 'This is My body, which is for you; do this in remembrance of Me.' In the same way He took the cup also after supper, saying, 'This cup is the new covenant in My blood; do this, as often as you drink it, in remembrance of Me.' For as often as you eat this bread and drink the cup, you proclaim the Lord's death until He comes" (1Co. 11:23-26).

## No One Can Say, "Jesus Is Lord," Except by the Holy Spirit

"Now concerning spiritual gifts, brethren, I do not want you to be unaware. You know that when you were pagans, you were led astray to the mute idols, however you were led. Therefore I make known to you that no one speaking by the Spirit of God says, 'Jesus is accursed'; and no one can say, 'Jesus is Lord,' except by the Holy Spirit" (1Co. 12:1-3).

### In Christ Jesus Our Lord

"Otherwise, what will those do who are baptized for the dead? If the dead are not raised at all, why then are they baptized for them? Why are we also in danger every hour? I affirm, brethren, by the boasting in you which I have in Christ Jesus our

Lord, I die daily. If from human motives I fought with wild beasts at Ephesus, what does it profit me? If the dead are not raised, LET US EAT AND DRINK, FOR TOMORROW WE DIE. Do not be deceived: 'Bad company corrupts good morals.' Become sober-minded as you ought, and stop sinning; for some have no knowledge of God. I speak this to your shame" (1Co. 15:29-34).

## But Thanks Be to God, Who Gives Us the Victory Through Our Lord Jesus Christ

"Now I say this, brethren, that flesh and blood cannot inherit the kingdom of God; nor does the perishable inherit the imperishable. Behold, I tell you a mystery; we will not all sleep, but we will all be changed, in a moment, in the twinkling of an eye, at the last trumpet; for the trumpet will sound, and the dead will be raised imperishable, and we will be changed. For this perishable must put on the imperishable, and this mortal must put on immortality. But when this perishable will have put on the imperishable, and this mortal will have put on immortality, then will come about the saying that is written, 'DEATH IS SWALLOWED UP in victory. O DEATH, WHERE IS YOUR VICTORY? O DEATH, WHERE IS YOUR STING?' The sting of death is sin, and the power of sin is the law; but thanks be to God, who gives us the victory through our Lord Jesus Christ" (1Co. 15:50-57).

# THE BOOK OF 2 CORINTHIANS

## Blessed Be the God and Father of Our Lord Jesus Christ

"Blessed be the God and Father of our Lord Jesus Christ, the Father of mercies and God of all comfort, who comforts us in all our affliction so that we will be able to comfort those who are in any affliction with the comfort with which we ourselves are comforted by God. For just as the sufferings of Christ are ours in abundance, so also our comfort is abundant through Christ. But if we are afflicted, it is for your comfort and salvation; or if we are comforted, it is for your comfort, which is effective in the patient enduring of the same sufferings which we also suffer; and our hope for you is firmly grounded, knowing that as you are sharers of our sufferings, so also you are sharers of our comfort" (2Co. 1:3-7).

## In the Day of Our Lord Jesus

"For our proud confidence is this: the testimony of our conscience, that in holiness and godly sincerity, not in fleshly wisdom but in the grace of God, we have conducted ourselves in the world, and especially toward you. For we write nothing else to you than what you read and understand, and I hope you will understand until the end; just as you also partially did understand us, that we are your reason to be proud as you also are ours, in the day of our Lord Jesus" (2Co. 1:12-14).

# The Son of God, Christ Jesus, Who Was Preached Among You by Us

"In this confidence I intended at first to come to you, so that you might twice receive a blessing; that is, to pass your way into Macedonia, and again from Macedonia to come to you, and by you to be helped on my journey to Judea. Therefore, I was not vacillating when I intended to do this, was I? Or what I purpose, do I purpose according to the flesh, so that with me there will be yes, yes and no, no at the same time? But as God is faithful, our word to you is not yes and no. For the Son of God, Christ Jesus, who was preached among you by us — by me and Silvanus and Timothy — was not yes and no, but is yes in Him. For as many as are the promises of God, in Him they are yes; therefore also through Him is our Amen to the glory of God through us. Now He who establishes us with you in Christ and anointed us is God, who also sealed us and gave us the Spirit in our hearts as a pledge" (2Co. 1:15-22).

## We Do Not Preach Ourselves but Christ Jesus as Lord

"Therefore, since we have this ministry, as we received mercy, we do not lose heart, but we have renounced the things hidden because of shame, not walking in craftiness or adulterating the word of God, but by the manifestation of truth commending ourselves to every man's conscience in the sight of God. And even if our gospel is veiled, it is veiled to those who are perishing, in whose case the god of this world has blinded the minds of the unbelieving so that they might not see the light of the gospel of the glory of Christ, who is the image of God. For we do not preach ourselves but Christ Jesus as Lord, and ourselves as your bond-servants for Jesus' sake. For God, who said, 'Light shall shine out of darkness,' is the One who has shone in our hearts to give the Light of the knowledge of the glory of God in the face of Christ" (2Co. 4:1-6).

## We Who Live Are Constantly Being Delivered Over to Death for Jesus' Sake

"But we have this treasure in earthen vessels, so that the surpassing greatness of the power will be of God and not from ourselves; we are afflicted in every way, but not crushed; perplexed, but not despairing; persecuted, but not forsaken; struck down, but not destroyed; always carrying about in the body the dying of Jesus, so that the life of Jesus also may be manifested in our body. For we who live are constantly being delivered over to death for Jesus' sake, so that the life of Jesus also may be manifested in our mortal flesh. So death works in us, but life in you" (2Co. 4:7-12).

## Knowing That He Who Raised the Lord Jesus Will Raise Us Also

"But having the same spirit of faith, according to what is written, 'I BELIEVED, THEREFORE I SPOKE,' we also believe, therefore we also speak, knowing that He who raised the Lord Jesus will raise us also with Jesus and will present us with you. For all things are for your sakes, so that the grace which is spreading to more and more people may cause the giving of thanks to abound to the glory of God" (2Co. 4:13-15).

## The Grace of Our Lord Jesus Christ

"But just as you abound in everything, in faith and utterance and knowledge and in all earnestness and in the love we inspired in you, see that you abound in this gracious work also. I am not speaking this as a command, but as proving through the earnestness of others the sincerity of your love also. For you know the grace of our Lord Jesus Christ, that though He was rich, yet for your sake He became poor, so that you through His poverty might become rich. I give my opinion in this matter, for this is to your advantage, who were the first to begin a year ago not only to do this, but also to desire to do it. But now finish doing it also, so that just as there was the readiness to desire it, so there may be also the completion of it by your ability. For if the readiness is present, it is acceptable according to what a person has, not according to what he does not have. For this is not for the ease of others and for your affliction, but by way of equality—at this present time your abundance being a supply for their need, so that their abundance also may become a supply for your need, that there may be equality; as it is written, 'HE WHO gathered MUCH DID NOT HAVE TOO MUCH, AND HE WHO gathered LITTLE HAD NO LACK'" (2Co. 8:7-15).

## Preaches Another Jesus Whom We Have Not Preached

"I wish that you would bear with me in a little foolishness; but indeed you are bearing with me. For I am jealous for you with a godly jealousy; for I betrothed you to one husband, so that to Christ I might present you as a pure virgin. But I am afraid that, as the serpent deceived Eve by his craftiness, your minds will be led astray from the simplicity and purity of devotion to Christ. For if one comes and preaches another Jesus whom we have not preached, or you receive a different spirit which you have not received, or a different gospel which you have not accepted, you bear this beautifully. For I consider myself not in the least inferior to the most eminent apostles. But even if I am unskilled in speech, yet I am not so in knowledge; in fact, in every way we have made this evident to you in all things" (2Co. 11:1-6).

## The Lord Jesus, Is Blessed Forever

"If I have to boast, I will boast of what pertains to my weakness. The God and Father of the Lord Jesus, He who is blessed forever, knows that I am not lying. In Damascus the ethnarch under Aretas the king was guarding the city of the Damascenes in order to seize me, and I was let down in a basket through a window in the wall, and so escaped his hands" (2Co. 11:30-33).

*Chapter Three*

# Do You Not Recognize This About Yourselves, that Jesus Christ Is in You

"Test yourselves to see if you are in the faith; examine yourselves! Or do you not recognize this about yourselves, that Jesus Christ is in you — unless indeed you fail the test? But I trust that you will realize that we ourselves do not fail the test. Now we pray to God that you do no wrong; not that we ourselves may appear approved, but that you may do what is right, even though we may appear unapproved. For we can do nothing against the truth, but only for the truth. For we rejoice when we ourselves are weak but you are strong; this we also pray for, that you be made complete. For this reason I am writing these things while absent, so that when present I need not use severity, in accordance with the authority which the Lord gave me for building up and not for tearing down" (2Co. 13:5-10).

## THE BOOK OF GALATIANS

## Peace from God Our Father, and the Lord Jesus Christ

"Grace to you and peace from God our Father and the Lord Jesus Christ, who gave Himself for our sins so that He might rescue us from this present evil age, according to the will of our God and Father, to whom be the glory forevermore. Amen" (Gal. 1:3-5).

# I Received It Through a Revelation of Jesus Christ

"For I would have you know, brethren, that the gospel which was preached by me is not according to man. For I neither received it from man, nor was I taught it, but I received it through a revelation of Jesus Christ" (Gal. 1:11-12).

## To Spy Out Our Liberty Which We Have in Christ Jesus

"Then after an interval of fourteen years I went up again to Jerusalem with Barnabas, taking Titus along also. It was because of a revelation that I went up; and I submitted to them the gospel which I preach among the Gentiles, but I did so in private to those who were of reputation, for fear that I might be running, or had run, in vain. But not even Titus, who was with me, though he was a Greek, was compelled to be circumcised. But it was because of the false brethren secretly brought in, who had sneaked in to spy out our liberty which we have in Christ Jesus, in order to bring us into bondage. But we did not yield in subjection to them for even an hour, so that the truth of the gospel would remain with you. But from those who were of high reputation (what they were makes no difference to me; God shows no partiality)—well, those who were of reputation contributed nothing to me. But on the contrary, seeing that I had been entrusted with the gospel to the uncircumcised, just as Peter had been to the circumcised (for He who effectually worked for Peter in his apostleship to the circumcised effectually worked for me also to the Gentiles), and recognizing the grace that had been given to me, James and Cephas and John, who were reputed to be pillars, gave to me and Barnabas the right hand of fellowship, so that we might go to the Gentiles and they to the circumcised. They only asked us to remember the poor—the very thing I also was eager to do" (Gal. 2:1-10).

## Through Faith in Christ Jesus

"We are Jews by nature and not sinners from among the Gentiles; nevertheless knowing that a man is not justified by the works of the Law but through faith in Christ Jesus, even we have believed in Christ Jesus, so that we may be justified by faith in Christ and not by the works of the Law; since by the works of the Law no flesh will be justified. But if, while seeking to be justified in Christ, we ourselves have also been found sinners, is Christ then a minister of sin? May it never be! For if I rebuild what I have once destroyed, I prove myself to be a transgressor. For through the Law I died to the Law, so that I might live to God. I have been crucified with Christ; and it is no longer I who live, but Christ lives in me; and the life which I now live in the flesh I live by faith in the Son of God, who loved me and gave Himself up for me. I do not nullify the grace of God, for if righteousness comes through the Law, then Christ died needlessly" (Gal. 2:15-21).

## Jesus Christ Was Publicly Portrayed

"You foolish Galatians, who has bewitched you, before whose eyes Jesus Christ was publicly portrayed as crucified? This is the only thing I want to find out from you: did you receive the Spirit by the works of the Law, or by hearing with faith? Are you so foolish? Having begun by the Spirit, are you now being perfected by the flesh? Did you suffer so many things in vain—if indeed it was in vain? So then, does He who provides you with the Spirit and works miracles among you, do it by the works of the Law, or by hearing with faith" (Gal. 3:1-5)?

## In Christ Jesus the Blessing of Abraham Might Come to the Gentiles

"For as many as are of the works of the Law are under a curse; for it is written, 'CURSED IS EVERYONE WHO DOES NOT ABIDE BY ALL THINGS WRITTEN IN THE BOOK OF THE LAW, TO PERFORM THEM.' Now that no one is justified by the Law before God is evident; for, 'THE RIGHTEOUS MAN SHALL LIVE BY FAITH.' However, the Law is not of faith; on the contrary, 'HE WHO PRACTICES THEM SHALL LIVE BY THEM.' Christ redeemed us from the curse of the Law, having become a curse for us—for it is written, 'CURSED IS EVERYONE WHO HANGS ON A TREE'—in order that in Christ Jesus the blessing of Abraham might come to the Gentiles, so that we would receive the promise of the Spirit through faith" (Gal. 3:10-14).

*Chapter Three*

# The Promise by Faith in Jesus Christ Might Be Given to Those Who Believe

"Why the Law then? It was added because of transgressions, having been ordained through angels by the agency of a mediator, until the seed would come to whom the promise had been made. Now a mediator is not for one party only; whereas God is only one. Is the Law then contrary to the promises of God? May it never be! For if a law had been given which was able to impart life, then righteousness would indeed have been based on law. But the Scripture has shut up everyone under sin, so that the promise by faith in Jesus Christ might be given to those who believe" (Gal. 3:19-22).

## For You Are All Sons of God Through Faith in Christ Jesus

"But before faith came, we were kept in custody under the law, being shut up to the faith which was later to be revealed. Therefore the Law has become our tutor to lead us to Christ, so that we may be justified by faith. But now that faith has come, we are no longer under a tutor. For you are all sons of God through faith in Christ Jesus. For all of you who were baptized into Christ have clothed yourselves with Christ. There is neither Jew nor Greek, there is neither slave nor free man, there is neither male nor female; for you are all one in Christ Jesus. And if you belong to Christ, then you are Abraham's descendants, heirs according to promise" (Gal. 3:23-29).

## As Christ Jesus Himself

"I beg of you, brethren, become as I am, for I also have become as you are. You have done me no wrong; but you know that it was because of a bodily illness that I preached the gospel to you the first time; and that which was a trial to you in my bodily condition you did not despise or loathe, but you received me as an angel of God, as Christ Jesus Himself. Where then is that sense of blessing you had? For I bear you witness that, if possible, you would have plucked out your eyes and given them to me. So have I become your enemy by telling you the truth? They eagerly seek you, not commendably, but they wish to shut you out so that you will seek them. But it is good always to be eagerly sought in a commendable manner, and not only when I am present with you. My children, with whom I am again in labor until Christ is formed in you—but I could wish to be present with you now and to change my tone, for I am perplexed about you" (Gal. 4:12-20).

## For In Christ Jesus Neither Circumcision nor Uncircumcision Means Anything

"Behold I, Paul, say to you that if you receive circumcision, Christ will be of no benefit to you. And I testify again to every man who receives circumcision, that he is under obligation to keep the whole Law. You have been severed from Christ, you who are seeking to be justified by law; you have fallen from grace. For we through the Spirit, by faith, are waiting for the hope of righteousness. For in

Christ Jesus neither circumcision nor uncircumcision means anything, but faith working through love" (Gal. 5:2-6).

## Those Who Belong to Christ Jesus Have Crucified the Flesh

"But I say, walk by the Spirit, and you will not carry out the desire of the flesh. For the flesh sets its desire against the Spirit, and the Spirit against the flesh; for these are in opposition to one another, so that you may not do the things that you please. But if you are led by the Spirit, you are not under the Law. Now the deeds of the flesh are evident, which are: immorality, impurity, sensuality, idolatry, sorcery, enmities, strife, jealousy, outbursts of anger, disputes, dissensions, factions, envying, drunkenness, carousing, and things like these, of which I forewarn you, just as I have forewarned you, that those who practice such things will not inherit the kingdom of God. But the fruit of the Spirit is love, joy, peace, patience, kindness, goodness, faithfulness, gentleness, self-control; against such things there is no law. Now those who belong to Christ Jesus have crucified the flesh with its passions and desires" (Gal. 5:16-24).

## In the Cross of Our Lord Jesus Christ

"See with what large letters I am writing to you with my own hand. Those who desire to make a good showing in the flesh try to compel you to be circumcised, simply so that they will not be persecuted for the cross of Christ. For those who are circumcised do not even keep the Law themselves, but they desire to have you circumcised so that they may boast in your flesh. But may it never be that I would boast, except in the cross of our Lord Jesus Christ, through which the world has been crucified to me, and I to the world. For neither is circumcision anything, nor uncircumcision, but a new creation. And those who will walk by this rule, peace and mercy be upon them, and upon the Israel of God" (Gal. 6:11-16).

## I Bear on My Body the Brand-Marks of Jesus

"From now on let no one cause trouble for me, for I bear on my body the brand-marks of Jesus. The grace of our Lord Jesus Christ be with your spirit, brethren. Amen" (Gal. 6:17-18).

## THE BOOK OF EPHESIANS

## He Predestined Us to Adoption as Sons Through Jesus Christ to Himself

"Blessed be the God and Father of our Lord Jesus Christ, who has blessed us with every spiritual blessing in the heavenly places in Christ, just as He chose us in Him before the foundation of the world, that we would be holy and blameless before Him. In love He predestined us to adoption as sons through Jesus Christ to Himself, according to the kind intention of His will, to the praise of the glory of His grace, which He freely bestowed on us in the Beloved. In Him we have redemption through His blood, the forgiveness of our trespasses, according to the riches of His grace which He lavished on us. In all wisdom and insight He made known to us the mystery of His will, according to His kind intention which He purposed in Him with a view to an administration suitable to the fullness of the times, that is, the summing up of all things in Christ, things in the heavens and things on the earth. In Him also we have obtained an inheritance, having been predestined according to His purpose who works all things after the counsel of His will, to the end that we who were the first to hope in Christ would be to the praise of His glory. In Him, you also, after listening to the message of truth, the gospel of your salvation—having also believed, you were sealed in Him with the Holy Spirit of promise, who is given as a pledge of our inheritance, with a view to the redemption of God's own possession, to the praise of His glory" (Eph. 1:3-14).

## Having Heard of the Faith in the Lord Jesus

"For this reason I too, having heard of the faith in the Lord Jesus which exists among you and your love for all the saints, do not cease giving thanks for you, while making mention of you in my prayers; that the God of our Lord Jesus Christ, the Father of glory, may give to you a spirit of wisdom and of revelation in the knowledge of Him. I pray that the eyes of your heart may be enlightened, so that you will know what is the hope of His calling, what are the riches of the glory of His inheritance in the saints, and what is the surpassing greatness of His power toward us who believe. These are in accordance with the working of the strength of His might which He brought about in Christ, when He raised Him from the dead and seated Him at His right hand in the heavenly places, far above all rule and authority and power and dominion, and every name that is named, not only in this age but also in the one to come. And He put all things in subjection under His feet, and gave Him as head over all things to the church, which is His body, the fullness of Him who fills all in all" (Eph. 1:15-23).

## Seated Us with Him in the Heavenly Places, in Christ Jesus

"And you were dead in your trespasses and sins, in which you formerly walked according to the course of this world, according to the prince of the power of the air, of the spirit that is now working in the sons of disobedience. Among them we too all formerly lived in the lusts of our flesh, indulging the desires of the flesh and of the mind, and were by nature children of wrath, even as the rest. But God, being rich in mercy, because of His great love with which He loved us, even when we were dead in our transgressions, made us alive together with Christ (by grace you have been saved), and raised us up with Him, and seated us with Him in the heavenly places in Christ Jesus, so that in the ages to come He might show the surpassing riches of His grace in kindness toward us in Christ Jesus. For by grace you have been saved through faith; and that not of yourselves, it is the gift of God; not as a result of works, so that no one may boast. For we are His workmanship, created in Christ Jesus for good works, which God prepared beforehand so that we would walk in them" (Eph. 2:1-10).

## You Who Formerly Were Far Off Have Been Brought Near by the Blood of Christ

"Therefore remember that formerly you, the Gentiles in the flesh, who are called 'Uncircumcision' by the so-called 'Circumcision,' which is performed in the flesh by human hands — remember that you were at that time separate from Christ, excluded from the commonwealth of Israel, and strangers to the covenants of promise, having no hope and without God in the world. But now in Christ Jesus you who formerly were far off have been brought near by the blood of Christ. For He Himself is our peace, who made both groups into one and broke down the barrier of the dividing wall, by abolishing in His flesh the enmity, which is the Law of commandments contained in ordinances, so that in Himself He might make the two into one new man, thus establishing peace, and might reconcile them both in one body to God through the cross, by it having put to death the enmity. AND HE CAME AND PREACHED PEACE TO YOU WHO WERE FAR AWAY, AND PEACE TO THOSE WHO WERE NEAR; for through Him we both have our access in one Spirit to the Father. So then you are no longer strangers and aliens, but you are fellow citizens with the saints, and are of God's household, having been built on the foundation of the apostles and prophets, Christ Jesus Himself being the corner stone, in whom the whole building, being fitted together, is growing into a holy temple in the Lord, in whom you also are being built together into a dwelling of

God in the Spirit" (Eph. 2:11-22).

## Fellow Partakers of the Promise in Christ Jesus through the Gospel

"For this reason I, Paul, the prisoner of Christ Jesus for the sake of you Gentiles—if indeed you have heard of the stewardship of God's grace which was given to me for you; that by revelation there was made known to me the mystery, as I wrote before in brief. By referring to this, when you read you can understand my insight into the mystery of Christ, which in other generations was not made known to the sons of men, as it has now been revealed to His holy apostles and prophets in the Spirit; to be specific, that the Gentiles are fellow heirs and fellow members of the body, and fellow partakers of the promise in Christ Jesus through the gospel, of which I was made a minister, according to the gift of God's grace which was given to me according to the working of His power. To me, the very least of all saints, this grace was given, to preach to the Gentiles the unfathomable riches of Christ, and to bring to light what is the administration of the mystery which for ages has been hidden in God who created all things; so that the manifold wisdom of God might now be made known through the church to the rulers and the authorities in the heavenly places. This was in accordance with the eternal purpose which He carried out in Christ Jesus our Lord, in whom we have boldness and confident access through faith in Him. Therefore I ask you not to lose heart at my tribulations on your behalf, for they are your glory"

*Chapter Three*

(Eph. 3:1-13).

## To Him Be the Glory in the Church and in Christ Jesus

"Now to Him who is able to do far more abundantly beyond all that we ask or think, according to the power that works within us, to Him be the glory in the church and in Christ Jesus to all generations forever and ever. Amen" (Eph. 3:20-21).

## Just as Truth Is in Jesus

"So this I say, and affirm together with the Lord, that you walk no longer just as the Gentiles also walk, in the futility of their mind, being darkened in their understanding, excluded from the life of God because of the ignorance that is in them, because of the hardness of their heart; and they, having become callous, have given themselves over to sensuality for the practice of every kind of impurity with greediness. But you did not learn Christ in this way, if indeed you have heard Him and have been taught in Him, just as truth is in Jesus, that, in reference to your former manner of life, you lay aside the old self, which is being corrupted in accordance with the lusts of deceit, and that you be renewed in the spirit of your mind, and put on the new self, which in the likeness of God has been created in righteousness and holiness of the truth" (Eph. 4:17-24).

## Always Giving Thanks for All Things in the Name of Our Lord Jesus Christ

"Therefore be careful how you walk, not as unwise men but as wise, making the most of your time, because the days are evil. So then do not be foolish, but understand what the will of the Lord is. And do not get drunk with wine, for that is dissipation, but be filled with the Spirit, speaking to one another in psalms and hymns and spiritual songs, singing and making melody with your heart to the Lord; always giving thanks for all things in the name of our Lord Jesus Christ to God, even the Father; and be subject to one another in the fear of Christ" (Eph. 5:15-21).

## All Those Who Love Our Lord Jesus Christ with a Love Incorruptible

"Peace be to the brethren, and love with faith, from God the Father and the Lord Jesus Christ. Grace be with all those who love our Lord Jesus Christ with incorruptible love" (Eph. 6:23-24).

.

## THE BOOK OF PHILIPPIANS

## He Who Began a Good Work in You Will Perfect It Until the Day of Christ Jesus

"I thank my God in all my remembrance of you, always offering prayer with joy in my every prayer for you all, in view of your participation in the gospel from the first day until now. For I am confident of this very thing, that He who began a good work in you will perfect it until the day of Christ Jesus. For it is only right for me to feel this way about you all, because I have you in my heart, since both in my imprisonment and in the defense and confirmation of the gospel, you all are partakers of grace with me. For God is my witness, how I long for you all with the affection of Christ Jesus. And this I pray, that your love may abound still more and more in real knowledge and all discernment, so that you may approve the things that are excellent, in order to be sincere and blameless until the day of Christ; having been filled with the fruit of righteousness which comes through Jesus Christ, to the glory and praise of God" (Php. 1:3-11).

## Through Your Prayers and the Provision of the Spirit of Jesus Christ

"Now I want you to know, brethren, that my circumstances have turned out for the greater progress of the gospel, so that my imprisonment in the cause of Christ has become well known throughout the whole praetorian guard and to everyone else, and that most of the brethren, trusting in the Lord because of my imprisonment, have far more courage to speak the word of God without fear. Some, to be sure, are preaching Christ even from envy and strife, but some also from good will; the latter do it out of love, knowing that I am appointed for the defense of the gospel; the former proclaim Christ out of selfish ambition rather than from pure motives, thinking to cause me distress in my imprisonment. What then? Only that in every way, whether in pretense or in truth, Christ is proclaimed; and in this I rejoice…" (Php. 1:12-18).

## In Christ Jesus

"Yes, and I will rejoice, for I know that this will turn out for my deliverance through your prayers and the provision of the Spirit of Jesus Christ, according to my earnest expectation and hope, that I will not be put to shame in anything, but that with all boldness, Christ will even now, as always, be exalted in my body, whether by life or by death. For to me, to live is Christ and to die is gain. But if I am to live on in the flesh, this will mean fruitful labor for me; and I do not know which to choose. But I am hard-pressed from both directions, having the desire to depart and be with Christ, for that is very much better; yet to remain on in the flesh is more necessary for your sake. Convinced of this, I know that I will remain and continue with you all for your progress and joy in the faith, so that your proud confidence in me may abound in Christ Jesus through my coming to you again" (Php. 1:18-26).

## At the Name of Jesus Every Knee Should Bow

"Therefore if there is any encouragement in Christ, if there is any consolation of love, if there is any fellowship of the Spirit, if any affection and compassion, make my joy complete by being of the same mind, maintaining the same love, united in spirit, intent on one purpose. Do nothing from selfishness or empty conceit, but with humility of mind regard one another as more important than yourselves; do not merely look out for your own personal interests, but also for the interests of others. Have this attitude in yourselves which was also in Christ Jesus, who, although He existed in the form of God, did not regard equality with God a thing to be grasped, but emptied Himself, taking the form of a bond-servant, and being made in the likeness of men. Being found in appearance as a man, He humbled Himself by becoming obedient to the point of death, even death on a cross. For this reason also, God highly exalted Him, and bestowed on Him the name which is above every name, so that at the name of Jesus EVERY KNEE WILL BOW, of those who are in heaven and on earth and under the earth, and that every tongue will confess that Jesus Christ is Lord, to the glory of God the Father" (Php. 2:1-11).

## They All Seek After Their Own Interests, Not Those of Christ Jesus

"But I hope in the Lord Jesus to send Timothy to you shortly, so that I also may be encouraged when I learn of your condition. For I have no one else of kindred spirit who will genuinely be concerned for your welfare. For they all seek after their own interests, not those of Christ Jesus. But you know of his proven worth, that he served with me in the furtherance of the gospel like a child serving his father. Therefore I hope to send him immediately, as soon as I see how things go with me; and I trust in the Lord that I myself also will be coming shortly. But I thought it necessary to send to you Epaphroditus, my brother and fellow worker and fellow soldier, who is also your messenger and minister to my need; because he was longing for you all and was distressed because you had heard that he was sick. For indeed he was sick to the point of death, but God had mercy on him, and not on him only but also on me, so that I would not have sorrow upon sorrow. Therefore I have sent him all the more eagerly so that when you see him again you may rejoice and I may be less concerned about you. Receive him then in the Lord with all joy, and hold men like him in high regard; because he came close to death for the work of Christ, risking his life to complete what was deficient in your service to me" (Php. 2:19-30).

## We Worship in the Spirit of God and Glory in Christ Jesus and Put No Confidence in the Flesh

"Beware of the dogs, beware of the evil workers, beware of the false circumcision; for we are the true circumcision, who worship in the Spirit of God and glory in Christ Jesus and put no confidence in the flesh, although I myself might have confidence even in the flesh. If anyone else has a mind to put confidence in the flesh, I far more: circumcised the eighth day, of the nation of Israel, of the tribe of Benjamin, a Hebrew of Hebrews; as to the Law, a Pharisee; as to zeal, a persecutor of the church; as to the righteousness which is in the Law, found blameless" (Php. 3:2-6).

## I Count All Things to Be Loss in View of the Surpassing Value of Knowing Christ Jesus

"But whatever things were gain to me, those things I have counted as loss for the sake of Christ.

More than that, I count all things to be loss in view of the surpassing value of knowing Christ Jesus my Lord, for whom I have suffered the loss of all things, and count them but rubbish so that I may gain Christ, and may be found in Him, not having a righteousness of my own derived from the Law, but that which is through faith in Christ, the righteousness which comes from God on the basis of faith, that I may know Him and the power of His resurrection and the fellowship of His sufferings, being conformed to His death; in order that I may attain to the resurrection from the dead" (Php. 3:7-11).

## The Upward Call of God in Christ Jesus

"Not that I have already obtained it or have already become perfect, but I press on so that I may lay hold of that for which also I was laid hold of by Christ Jesus. Brethren, I do not regard myself as having laid hold of it yet; but one thing I do: forgetting what lies behind and reaching forward to what lies ahead, I press on toward the goal for the prize of the upward call of God in Christ Jesus. Let us therefore, as many as are perfect, have this attitude; and if in anything you have a different attitude, God will reveal that also to you; however, let us keep living by that same standard to which we have attained" (Php. 3:12-16).

## We Eagerly Wait for a Savior, the Lord Jesus Christ

"Brethren, join in following my example, and observe those who walk according to the pattern you have in us. For many walk, of whom I often told you, and now tell you even weeping, that they are enemies of the cross of Christ, whose end is destruction, whose god is their appetite, and whose glory is in their shame, who set their minds on earthly things. For our citizenship is in heaven, from which also we eagerly wait for a Savior, the Lord Jesus Christ; who will transform the body of our humble state into conformity with the body of His glory, by the exertion of the power that He has even to subject all things to Himself" (Php. 3:17-21).

## The Peace of God, Shall Guard Your Hearts and Your Minds in Christ Jesus

"Rejoice in the Lord always; again I will say, rejoice! Let your gentle spirit be known to all men. The Lord is near. Be anxious for nothing, but in everything by prayer and supplication with thanksgiving let your requests be made known to God. And the peace of God, which surpasses all comprehension, will guard your hearts and your minds in Christ Jesus" (Php. 4:4-7).

## God Shall Supply All Your Needs According to His Riches in Glory in Christ Jesus

"You yourselves also know, Philippians, that at the first preaching of the gospel, after I left Macedonia, no church shared with me in the matter of giving and receiving but you alone; for even in Thessalonica you sent a gift more than once for my needs. Not that I seek the gift itself, but I seek for the profit which increases to your account. But I have received everything in full and have an abundance; I am amply supplied, having received from Epaphroditus what you have sent, a fragrant aroma, an acceptable sacrifice, well-pleasing to God. And my God will supply all your needs according to His riches in glory in Christ Jesus. Now to our God and Father be the glory forever and ever. Amen" (Php. 4:15-20).

## THE BOOK OF COLOSSIANS

### Your Faith in Christ Jesus and the Love which You Have for All the Saints

"We give thanks to God, the Father of our Lord Jesus Christ, praying always for you, since we heard of your faith in Christ Jesus and the love which you have for all the saints; because of the hope laid up for you in heaven, of which you previously heard in the word of truth, the gospel which has come to you, just as in all the world also it is constantly bearing fruit and increasing, even as it has been doing in you also since the day you heard of it and understood the grace of God in truth; just as you learned it from Epaphras, our beloved fellow bond-servant, who is a faithful servant of Christ on our behalf, and he also informed us of your love in the Spirit" (Col. 1:3-8).

### You Therefore Have Received Christ Jesus the Lord, so Walk in Him

"Therefore as you have received Christ Jesus the Lord, so walk in Him, having been firmly rooted and now being built up in Him and established in your faith, just as you were instructed, and overflowing with gratitude" (Col. 2:6-7).

## Do It All in the Name of the Lord Jesus

"So, as those who have been chosen of God, holy and beloved, put on a heart of compassion, kindness, humility, gentleness and patience; bearing with one another, and forgiving each other, whoever has a complaint against anyone; just as the Lord forgave you, so also should you. Beyond all these things put on love, which is the perfect bond of unity. Let the peace of Christ rule in your hearts, to which indeed you were called in one body; and be thankful. Let the word of Christ richly dwell within you, with all wisdom teaching and admonishing one another with psalms and hymns and spiritual songs, singing with thankfulness in your hearts to God. Whatever you do in word or deed, do all in the name of the Lord Jesus, giving thanks through Him to God the Father" (Col. 3:12-17).

## A Bondslave of Jesus Christ

"Aristarchus, my fellow prisoner, sends you his greetings; and also Barnabas's cousin Mark (about whom you received instructions; if he comes to you, welcome him); and also Jesus who is called Justus; these are the only fellow workers for the kingdom of God who are from the circumcision, and they have proved to be an encouragement to me. Epaphras, who is one of your number, a bondslave of Jesus Christ, sends you his greetings, always laboring earnestly for you in his prayers, that you may stand perfect and fully assured in all the will of God. For I testify for him that he has a deep concern for you and for those who are in Laodicea and Hierapolis. Luke, the beloved physician, sends you his greetings, and also Demas. Greet the brethren who are in Laodicea and also Nympha and the church that is in her house. When this letter is read among you, have it also read in the church of the Laodiceans; and you, for your part read my letter that is coming from Laodicea. Say to Archippus, "Take heed to the ministry which you have received in the Lord, that you may fulfill it" (Col. 4:10-17).

.

## THE BOOK OF 1 THESSALONIANS

### Your Labor of Love and Steadfastness of Hope in Our Lord Jesus

"We give thanks to God always for all of you, making mention of you in our prayers; constantly bearing in mind your work of faith and labor of love and steadfastness of hope in our Lord Jesus Christ in the presence of our God and Father, knowing, brethren beloved by God, His choice of you; for our gospel did not come to you in word only, but also in power and in the Holy Spirit and with full conviction; just as you know what kind of men we proved to be among you for your sake. You also became imitators of us and of the Lord, having received the word in much tribulation with the joy of the Holy Spirit, so that you became an example to all the believers in Macedonia and in Achaia. For the word of the Lord has sounded forth from you, not only in Macedonia and Achaia, but also in every place your faith toward God has gone forth, so that we have no need to say anything. For they themselves report about us what kind of a reception we had with you, and how you turned to God from idols to serve a living and true God, and to wait for His Son from heaven, whom He raised from the dead, that is Jesus, who rescues us from the wrath to come" (1Th. 1:2-10).

## For You, Brethren, Became Imitators of the Churches of God in Christ Jesus

"For this reason we also constantly thank God that when you received the word of God which you heard from us, you accepted it not as the word of men, but for what it really is, the word of God, which also performs its work in you who believe. For you, brethren, became imitators of the churches of God in Christ Jesus that are in Judea, for you also endured the same sufferings at the hands of your own countrymen, even as they did from the Jews, who both killed the Lord Jesus and the prophets, and drove us out. They are not pleasing to God, but hostile to all men, hindering us from speaking to the Gentiles so that they may be saved; with the result that they always fill up the measure of their sins. But wrath has come upon them to the utmost" (1Th. 2:13-16).

## In the Presence of Our Lord Jesus at His Coming

"But we, brethren, having been taken away from you for a short while—in person, not in spirit—

were all the more eager with great desire to see your face. For we wanted to come to you — I, Paul, more than once — and yet Satan hindered us. For who is our hope or joy or crown of exultation? Is it not even you, in the presence of our Lord Jesus at His coming? For you are our glory and joy" (1Th. 2:17-20).

## May Jesus Our Lord Direct Our Way to You

"Now may our God and Father Himself and Jesus our Lord direct our way to you; and may the Lord cause you to increase and abound in love for one another, and for all people, just as we also do for you; so that He may establish your hearts without blame in holiness before our God and Father at the coming of our Lord Jesus with all His saints" (1Th. 3:11-13).

## You Know What Commandments We Gave You by the Authority of the Lord Jesus

"Finally then, brethren, we request and exhort you in the Lord Jesus, that as you received from us instruction as to how you ought to walk and please God (just as you actually do walk), that you excel still more. For you know what commandments we gave you by the authority of the Lord Jesus. For this is the will of God, your sanctification; that is, that you abstain from sexual immorality; that each of you know how to possess his own vessel in sanctification and honor, not in lustful passion, like the Gentiles who do not know God; and that no man transgress and defraud his brother in the matter because the Lord is the avenger in all these things, just as we also told you before and solemnly warned you. For God has not called us for the purpose of impurity, but in sanctification. So, he who rejects this is not rejecting man but the God who gives His Holy Spirit to you" (1Th. 4:1-8).

## We Believe that Jesus Died and Rose Again

"But we do not want you to be uninformed, brethren, about those who are asleep, so that you will not grieve as do the rest who have no hope. For if we believe that Jesus died and rose again, even so God will bring with Him those who have fallen asleep in Jesus. For this we say to you by the word of the Lord, that we who are alive and remain until the coming of the Lord, will not precede those who have fallen asleep. For the Lord Himself will descend from heaven with a shout, with the voice of the archangel and with the trumpet of God, and the dead in Christ will rise first. Then we who are alive and remain will be caught up together with them in the clouds to meet the Lord in the air, and so we shall always be with the Lord. Therefore comfort one another with these words" (1Th. 4:13-18).

## Obtaining Salvation Through Our Lord Jesus Christ

"Now as to the times and the epochs, brethren, you have no need of anything to be written to you. For you yourselves know full well that the day of the Lord will come just like a thief in the night. While they are saying, 'Peace and safety!' then destruction will come upon them suddenly like labor pains upon a woman with child, and they will not escape. But you, brethren, are not in darkness, that the day would overtake you like a thief; for you are all sons of light and sons of day. We are not of night nor of darkness; so then let us not sleep as others do, but let us be alert and sober. For those who sleep do their sleeping at night, and those who get drunk get drunk at night. But since we are of the day, let us be sober, having put on the breastplate of faith and love, and as a helmet, the hope of salvation. For God has not destined us for wrath, but for obtaining salvation through our Lord Jesus Christ, who died for us, so that whether we are awake or asleep, we will live together with Him. Therefore encourage one another and build up one another, just as you also are doing" (1Th. 5:1-11).

## In Everything Give Thanks; for This Is God's Will for You in Christ Jesus

"But we request of you, brethren, that you appreciate those who diligently labor among you, and have charge over you in the Lord and give you instruction, and that you esteem them very highly in love because of their work. Live in peace with one another. We urge you, brethren, admonish the unruly, encourage the fainthearted, help the weak, be patient with everyone. See that no one repays another with evil for evil, but always seek after that which is good for one another and for all people. Rejoice always; pray without ceasing; in everything give thanks; for this is God's will for you in Christ Jesus. Do not quench the Spirit; do not despise prophetic utterances. But examine everything carefully; hold fast to that which is good; abstain from every form of evil" (1Th. 5:12-22).

## Preserved Complete, Without Blame at the Coming of Our Lord Jesus Christ

"Now may the God of peace Himself sanctify you entirely; and may your spirit and soul and body be preserved complete, without blame at the coming of our Lord Jesus Christ. Faithful is He who calls you, and He also will bring it to pass" (1Th. 5:23-24).

## THE BOOK OF 2 THESSALONIANS

## When the Lord Jesus Shall Be Revealed from Heaven with His Mighty Angels

"We ought always to give thanks to God for you, brethren, as is only fitting, because your faith is greatly enlarged, and the love of each one of you toward one another grows ever greater; therefore, we ourselves speak proudly of you among the churches of God for your perseverance and faith in the midst of all your persecutions and afflictions which you endure. This is a plain indication of God's righteous judgment so that you will be considered worthy of the kingdom of God, for which indeed you are suffering. For after all it is only just for God to repay with affliction those who afflict you, and to give relief to you who are afflicted and to us as well when the Lord Jesus will be revealed from heaven with His mighty angels in flaming fire, dealing out retribution to those who do not know God and to those who do not obey the gospel of our Lord Jesus. These will pay the penalty of eternal destruction, away from the presence of the Lord and from the glory of His power, when He comes to be glorified in His saints on that day, and to be marveled at among all who have believed—for our testimony to you was believed. To this end also we pray for you always, that our God will count you worthy of your calling, and fulfill every desire for goodness and the work of faith with power, so that the name of our Lord Jesus will be glorified in you, and you in Him, according to the grace of our God and the Lord Jesus Christ" (2Th. 1:3-12).

## With Regard to the Coming of Our Lord Jesus Christ

"Now we request you, brethren, with regard to the coming of our Lord Jesus Christ and our gathering together to Him, that you not be quickly shaken from your composure or be disturbed either by a spirit or a message or a letter as if from us, to the effect that the day of the Lord has come. Let no one in any way deceive you, for it will not come unless the apostasy comes first, and the man of lawlessness is revealed, the son of destruction, who opposes and exalts himself above every so-called god or object of worship, so that he takes his seat in the temple of God, displaying himself as being God. Do you not remember that while I was still with you, I was telling you these things? And you know what restrains him now, so that in his time he will be revealed. For the mystery of lawlessness is already at work; only he who now restrains will do so until he is taken out of the way. Then that lawless one will be revealed whom the Lord will slay with the breath of His mouth and bring to an end by the appearance of His coming; that is, the one whose coming is in accord with the activity of Satan, with all power and signs and false wonders, and with all the deception of wickedness for those who perish, because they did not receive the love of the truth so as to be saved. For this reason God will send upon them a deluding influence so that they will believe what is false, in order that they all may be judged who did not believe the truth, but took pleasure in wickedness" (2Th. 2:1-12).

## That You May Gain the Glory of Our Lord Jesus Christ

"But we should always give thanks to God for you, brethren beloved by the Lord, because God has chosen you from the beginning for salvation through sanctification by the Spirit and faith in the truth. It was for this He called you through our gospel, that you may gain the glory of our Lord Jesus Christ. So then, brethren, stand firm and hold to the traditions which you were taught, whether by word of mouth or by letter from us" (2Th. 2:13-15).

## In the Name of Our Lord Jesus Christ

"Now we command you, brethren, in the name of our Lord Jesus Christ, that you keep away from every brother who leads an unruly life and not according to the tradition which you received from us. For you yourselves know how you ought to follow our example, because we did not act in an undisciplined manner among you, nor did we eat anyone's bread without paying for it, but with labor and hardship we kept working night and day so that we would not be a burden to any of you; not because we do not have the right to this, but in order to offer ourselves as a model for you, so that you would follow our example. For even when we were with you, we used to give you this order: if anyone is not willing to work, then he is not to eat, either. For we hear that some among you are leading an undisciplined life, doing no work at all, but acting like busybodies. Now such persons we command and exhort in the Lord Jesus Christ to work in quiet fashion and eat their own bread. But as for you, brethren, do not grow weary of doing good" (2Th. 3:6-13).

## THE BOOK OF 1 TIMOTHY

### The Faith and Love Which Are Found in Christ Jesus

"I thank Christ Jesus our Lord, who has strengthened me, because He considered me faithful, putting me into service, even though I was formerly a blasphemer and a persecutor and a violent aggressor. Yet I was shown mercy because I acted ignorantly in unbelief; and the grace of our Lord was more than abundant, with the faith and love which are found in Christ Jesus. It is a trustworthy statement, deserving full acceptance, that Christ Jesus came into the world to save sinners, among whom I am foremost of all. Yet for this reason I found mercy, so that in me as the foremost, Jesus Christ might demonstrate His perfect patience as an example for those who would believe in Him for eternal life. Now to the King eternal, immortal, invisible, the only God, be honor and glory forever and ever. Amen" (1Ti. 1:12-17).

## One Mediator Also Between God and Men, the Man Christ Jesus

"First of all, then, I urge that entreaties and prayers, petitions and thanksgivings, be made on behalf of all men, for kings and all who are in authority, so that we may lead a tranquil and quiet life in all godliness and dignity. This is good and acceptable in the sight of God our Savior, who desires all men to be saved and to come to the knowledge of the truth. For there is one God, and one mediator also between God and men, the man Christ Jesus, who gave Himself as a ransom for all, the testimony given at the proper time. For this I was appointed a preacher and an apostle (I am telling the truth, I am not lying) as a teacher of the Gentiles in faith and truth" (1Ti. 2:1-7).

## Great Confidence in the Faith that Is in Christ Jesus

"Deacons likewise must be men of dignity, not double-tongued, or addicted to much wine or fond of sordid gain, but holding to the mystery of the faith with a clear conscience. These men must also first be tested; then let them serve as deacons if they are beyond reproach. Women must likewise be dignified, not malicious gossips, but temperate, faithful in all things. Deacons must be husbands of only one wife, and good managers of their children and their own households. For those who have served well as deacons obtain for themselves a high standing and great confidence in the faith that is in Christ Jesus" (1Ti. 3:8-13).

## You Will Be a Good Servant of Christ Jesus

"In pointing out these things to the brethren, you will be a good servant of Christ Jesus, constantly nourished on the words of the faith and of the sound doctrine which you have been following. But have nothing to do with worldly fables fit only for old women. On the other hand, discipline yourself for the purpose of godliness; for bodily discipline is only of little profit, but godliness is profitable for all things, since it holds promise for the present life and also for the life to come. It is a trustworthy statement deserving full acceptance. For it is for this we labor and strive, because we have fixed our hope on the living God, who is the Savior of all men, especially of believers" (1Ti. 4:6-10).

## In the Presence of God and of Christ Jesus and of His Chosen Angels

"The elders who rule well are to be considered worthy of double honor, especially those who work hard at preaching and teaching. For the Scripture says, 'YOU SHALL NOT MUZZLE THE OX WHILE HE IS THRESHING,' and 'The laborer is worthy of his wages.' Do not receive an accusation against an elder except on the basis of two or three witnesses. Those who continue in sin, rebuke in the presence of all, so that the rest also will be fearful of sinning. I solemnly charge you in the presence of God and of Christ Jesus and of His chosen angels, to maintain these principles without bias, doing nothing in a spirit of partiality. Do not lay hands upon anyone too hastily and thereby share responsibility for the sins of others; keep yourself free from sin" (1Ti. 5:17-22).

## Those of Our Lord Jesus Christ

"If anyone advocates a different doctrine and does not agree with sound words, those of our Lord Jesus Christ, and with the doctrine conforming to godliness, he is conceited and understands nothing; but he has a morbid interest in controversial questions and disputes about words, out of which arise envy, strife, abusive language, evil suspicions, and constant friction between men of depraved mind and deprived of the truth, who suppose that godliness is a means of gain. But godliness actually is a means of great gain when accompanied by contentment. For we have brought nothing into the world, so we cannot take anything out of it either. If we have food and covering, with these we shall be content. But those who want to get rich fall into temptation and a snare and many foolish and harmful desires which plunge men into ruin and destruction. For the love of money is a root of all sorts of evil, and some by longing for it have wandered away from the faith and pierced themselves with many griefs" (1Ti. 6:3-10).

## Christ Jesus, Who Testified the Good Confession Before Pontius Pilate

"But flee from these things, you man of God, and pursue righteousness, godliness, faith, love, perseverance and gentleness. Fight the good fight of faith; take hold of the eternal life to which you were called, and you made the good confession in the presence of many witnesses. I charge you in the presence of God, who gives life to all things, and of Christ Jesus, who testified the good confession before Pontius Pilate, that you keep the commandment without stain or reproach until the appearing of our Lord Jesus Christ, which He will bring about at the proper time—He who is the blessed and only Sovereign, the King of kings and Lord of lords, who alone possesses immortality and dwells in unapproachable light, whom no man has seen or can see. To Him be honor and eternal dominion! Amen" (1Ti. 6:11-16).

## THE BOOK OF 2 TIMOTHY

### Granted Us in Christ Jesus from All Eternity

"Therefore do not be ashamed of the testimony of our Lord or of me His prisoner, but join with me in suffering for the gospel according to the power of God, who has saved us and called us with a holy calling, not according to our works, but according to His own purpose and grace which was granted us in Christ Jesus from all eternity, but now has been revealed by the appearing of our Savior Christ Jesus, who abolished death and brought life and immortality to light through the gospel, for which I was appointed a preacher and an apostle and a teacher. For this reason I also suffer these things, but I am not ashamed; for I know whom I have believed and I am convinced that He is able to guard what I have entrusted to Him until that day. Retain the standard of sound words which you have heard from me, in the faith and love which are in Christ Jesus. Guard, through the Holy Spirit who dwells in us, the treasure which has been entrusted to you" (2Ti. 1:8-14).

## Be Strong in the Grace that Is in Christ Jesus

"You therefore, my son, be strong in the grace that is in Christ Jesus. The things which you have heard from me in the presence of many witnesses, entrust these to faithful men who will be able to teach others also. Suffer hardship with me, as a good soldier of Christ Jesus. No soldier in active service entangles himself in the affairs of everyday life, so that he may please the one who enlisted him as a soldier. Also if anyone competes as an athlete, he does not win the prize unless he competes according to the rules. The hard-working farmer ought to be the first to receive his share of the crops. Consider what I say, for the Lord will give you understanding in everything" (2Ti. 2:1-7).

## Remember Jesus Christ, Risen from the Dead, Descendant of David

"Remember Jesus Christ, risen from the dead, descendant of David, according to my gospel, for which I suffer hardship even to imprisonment as a criminal; but the word of God is not imprisoned. For this reason I endure all things for the sake of those who are chosen, so that they also may obtain the salvation which is in Christ Jesus and with it eternal glory. It is a trustworthy statement: For if we died with Him, we will also live with Him; If we endure, we will also reign with Him; If we deny Him, He also will deny us; If we are faithless, He remains faithful, for He cannot deny Himself" (2Ti. 2:8-13).

## Who Desire to Live Godly in Christ Jesus Will Be Persecuted

"Now you followed my teaching, conduct, purpose, faith, patience, love, perseverance, persecutions, and sufferings, such as happened to me at Antioch, at Iconium and at Lystra; what persecutions I endured, and out of them all the Lord rescued me! Indeed, all who desire to live godly in Christ Jesus will be persecuted. But evil men and impostors will proceed from bad to worse, deceiving and being deceived. You, however, continue in the things you have learned and become convinced of, knowing from whom you have learned them, and that from childhood you have known the sacred writings which are able to give you the wisdom that leads to salvation through faith which is in Christ Jesus. All Scripture is inspired by God and profitable for teaching, for reproof, for correction, for training in righteousness; so that the man of God may be adequate, equipped for every good work" (2Ti. 3:10-17).

# Christ Jesus, Who Is to Judge the Living and the Dead

"I solemnly charge you in the presence of God and of Christ Jesus, who is to judge the living and the dead, and by His appearing and His kingdom: preach the word; be ready in season and out of season; reprove, rebuke, exhort, with great patience and instruction. For the time will come when they will not endure sound doctrine; but wanting to have their ears tickled, they will accumulate for themselves teachers in accordance to their own desires, and will turn away their ears from the truth and will turn aside to myths. But you, be sober in all things, endure hardship, do the work of an evangelist, fulfill your ministry" (2Ti. 4:1-5).

## THE BOOK OF TITUS

## An Apostle of Jesus Christ, for the faith of Those Chosen

"Paul, a bond-servant of God and an apostle of Jesus Christ, for the faith of those chosen of God and the knowledge of the truth which is according to godliness, in the hope of eternal life, which God, who cannot lie, promised long ages ago, but at the proper time manifested, even His word, in the proclamation with which I was entrusted according to the commandment of God our Savior" (Tit. 1:1-3).

*Chapter Three*

## Our Great God and Savior, Christ Jesus

"For the grace of God has appeared, bringing salvation to all men, instructing us to deny ungodliness and worldly desires and to live sensibly, righteously and godly in the present age, looking for the blessed hope and the appearing of the glory of our great God and Savior, Christ Jesus, who gave Himself for us to redeem us from every lawless deed, and to purify for Himself a people for His own possession, zealous for good deeds" (Tit. 2:11-14).

## He Poured Out upon Us Richly Through Jesus Christ Our Savior

"Remind them to be subject to rulers, to authorities, to be obedient, to be ready for every good deed, to malign no one, to be peaceable, gentle, showing every consideration for all men. For we also once were foolish ourselves, disobedient, deceived, enslaved to various lusts and pleasures, spending our life in malice and envy, hateful, hating one another. But when the kindness of God our Savior and His love for mankind appeared, He saved us, not on the basis of deeds which we have done in righteousness, but according to His mercy, by the washing of regeneration and renewing by the Holy Spirit, whom He poured out upon us richly through Jesus Christ our Savior, so that being justified by His grace we would be made heirs according to the hope of eternal life. This is a trustworthy statement; and concerning these things I want you to speak confidently, so that those who have believed God will be careful to engage in good deeds. These things are good and profitable for men. But avoid foolish controversies and genealogies and strife and disputes about the Law, for they are unprofitable and worthless. Reject a factious man after a first and second warning, knowing that such a man is perverted and is sinning, being self-condemned" (Tit. 3:1-11).

## THE BOOK OF PHILEMON

### A Prisoner of Christ Jesus

"I thank my God always, making mention of you in my prayers, because I hear of your love and of the faith which you have toward the Lord Jesus and toward all the saints; and I pray that the fellowship of your faith may become effective through the knowledge of every good thing which is in you for Christ's sake. For I have come to have much joy and comfort in your love, because the hearts of the saints have been refreshed through you, brother. Therefore, though I have enough confidence in Christ to order you to do what is proper, yet for love's sake I rather appeal to you — since I am such a person as Paul, the aged, and now also a prisoner of Christ Jesus" (Phm. 1:4-9).

## THE BOOK OF HEBREWS

### Jesus' Tasted Death for Everyone

"For He did not subject to angels the world to come, concerning which we are speaking. But one has testified somewhere, saying, 'WHAT IS MAN, THAT YOU REMEMBER HIM? OR THE SON OF MAN, THAT YOU ARE CONCERNED ABOUT HIM? YOU HAVE MADE HIM FOR A LITTLE WHILE LOWER THAN THE ANGELS; YOU HAVE CROWNED HIM WITH GLORY AND HONOR, AND HAVE APPOINTED HIM OVER THE WORKS OF YOUR HANDS; YOU HAVE PUT ALL THINGS IN SUBJECTION UNDER HIS FEET.' For in subjecting all things to him, He left nothing that is not subject to him. But now we do not yet see all things subjected to him. But we do see Him who was made for a little while lower than the angels, namely, Jesus, because of the suffering of death crowned with glory and honor, so that by the grace of God He might taste death for everyone. For it was fitting for Him, for whom are all things, and through whom are all things, in bringing many sons to glory, to perfect the author of their salvation through sufferings. For both He who sanctifies and those who are sanctified are all from one Father; for which reason He is not ashamed to call them brethren, saying, 'I WILL PROCLAIM YOUR NAME TO MY BRETHREN, IN THE MIDST OF THE CONGREGATION I WILL SING YOUR PRAISE.' And again, 'I WILL PUT MY TRUST IN HIM.' And again, 'BEHOLD, I AND THE CHILDREN WHOM GOD HAS GIVEN ME.' Therefore, since the children share in flesh and blood, He Himself likewise also partook of the same, that through death He might render powerless him who had the power of death, that is, the devil" (Heb. 2:5-14).

*Chapter Three*

# Consider Jesus, the Apostle and High Priest of Our Confession

"Therefore, holy brethren, partakers of a heavenly calling, consider Jesus, the Apostle and High Priest of our confession; He was faithful to Him who appointed Him, as Moses also was in all His house. For He has been counted worthy of more glory than Moses, by just so much as the builder of the house has more honor than the house. For every house is built by someone, but the builder of all things is God. Now Moses was faithful in all His house as a servant, for a testimony of those things which were to be spoken later; but Christ was faithful as a Son over His house—whose house we are, if we hold fast our confidence and the boast of our hope firm until the end" (Heb. 3:1-6).

## A Great High Priest, Jesus the Son of God

"Therefore, since we have a great high priest who has passed through the heavens, Jesus the Son of God, let us hold fast our confession. For we do not have a high priest who cannot sympathize with our weaknesses, but One who has been tempted in all things as we are, yet without sin. Therefore let us draw near with confidence to the throne of grace, so that we may receive mercy and find grace to help in time of need" (Heb. 4:14-16).

## Jesus Became a High Priest Forever According to the Order of Melchizedek

"For when God made the promise to Abraham, since He could swear by no one greater, He swore by Himself, saying, 'I WILL SURELY BLESS YOU AND I WILL SURELY MULTIPLY YOU.' And so, having patiently waited, he obtained the promise. For men swear by one greater than themselves, and with them an oath given as confirmation is an end of every dispute. In the same way God, desiring even more to show to the heirs of the promise the unchangeableness of His purpose, interposed with an oath, so that by two unchangeable things in which it is impossible for God to lie, we who have taken refuge would have strong encouragement to take hold of the hope set before us. This hope we have as an anchor of the soul, a hope both sure and steadfast and one which enters within the veil, where Jesus has entered as a forerunner for us, having become a high priest forever according to the order of Melchizedek" (Heb. 6:13-20).

## Jesus Has Become the Guarantee of a Better Covenant

"Now if perfection was through the Levitical priesthood (for on the basis of it the people received the Law), what further need was there for another priest to arise according to the order of Melchizedek, and not be designated according to the order of Aaron? For when the priesthood is changed, of necessity there takes place a change of law also. For the one concerning whom these things are spoken belongs to another tribe, from which no one has officiated at the altar. For it is evident that our Lord was descended from Judah, a tribe with reference to which Moses spoke nothing concerning priests. And this is clearer still, if another priest arises according to the likeness of Melchizedek, who has become such not on the basis of a law of physical requirement, but according to the power of an indestructible life. For it is attested of Him, 'YOU ARE A PRIEST FOREVER ACCORDING TO THE ORDER OF MELCHIZEDEK.' For, on the one hand, there is a setting aside of a former commandment because of its weakness and uselessness (for the Law made nothing perfect), and on the other hand there is a bringing in of a better hope, through which we draw near to God. And inasmuch as it was not without an oath (for they indeed became priests without an oath, but He with an oath through the One who said to Him, 'THE LORD HAS SWORN AND WILL NOT CHANGE HIS MIND, "YOU ARE A PRIEST FOREVER"'); so much the more also Jesus has become the guarantee of a better covenant" (Heb. 7:11-22).

## Jesus Christ Once for All

"For the Law, since it has only a shadow of the good things to come and not the very form of things, can never, by the same sacrifices which they offer continually year by year, make perfect those who draw near. Otherwise, would they not have ceased to be offered, because the worshipers, having once been cleansed, would no longer have had consciousness of sins? But in those sacrifices there is a reminder of sins year by year. For it is impossible for the blood of bulls and goats to take away sins. Therefore, when He comes into the world, He says, 'SACRIFICE AND OFFERING YOU HAVE NOT DESIRED, BUT A BODY YOU HAVE PREPARED FOR ME; IN WHOLE BURNT OFFERINGS AND sacrifices FOR SIN YOU HAVE TAKEN NO PLEASURE. THEN I SAID, "BEHOLD, I HAVE COME (IN THE SCROLL OF THE BOOK IT IS WRITTEN OF ME) TO DO YOUR WILL, O GOD."' After saying above, 'SACRIFICES AND OFFERINGS AND WHOLE BURNT OFFERINGS AND sacrifices FOR SIN YOU HAVE NOT DESIRED, NOR HAVE YOU TAKEN PLEASURE in them' (which are offered according to the Law), then He said, 'BEHOLD, I HAVE COME TO DO YOUR WILL.' He takes away the first in order to establish the second. By this will we have been sanctified through the offering of the body of Jesus Christ once for all" (Heb. 10:1-10).

## Confidence to Enter the Holy Place by the Blood of Jesus

"Therefore, brethren, since we have confidence to enter the holy place by the blood of Jesus, by a new and living way which He inaugurated for us through the veil, that is, His flesh, and since we have a great priest over the house of God, let us draw near with a sincere heart in full assurance of faith, having our hearts sprinkled clean from an evil conscience and our bodies washed with pure water. Let us hold fast the confession of our hope without wavering, for He who promised is faithful; and let us consider how to stimulate one another to love and good deeds, not forsaking our own assembling together, as is the habit of some, but encouraging one another; and all the more as you see the day drawing near" (Heb. 10:19-25).

## Fixing Our Eyes on Jesus, the Author and Perfecter of Faith

"Therefore, since we have so great a cloud of witnesses surrounding us, let us also lay aside every encumbrance and the sin which so easily entangles us, and let us run with endurance the race that is set before us, fixing our eyes on Jesus, the author and perfecter of faith, who for the joy set before Him endured the cross, despising the shame, and has sat down at the right hand of the throne of God" (Heb. 12:1-2).

## Jesus, the Mediator of a New Covenant

"For you have not come to a mountain that can be touched and to a blazing fire, and to darkness and gloom and whirlwind, and to the blast of a trumpet and the sound of words which sound was such that those who heard begged that no further word be spoken to them. For they could not bear the command, 'IF EVEN A BEAST TOUCHES THE MOUNTAIN, IT WILL BE STONED.' And so terrible was the sight, that Moses said, 'I AM FULL OF FEAR and trembling.' But you have come to Mount Zion and to the city of the living God, the heavenly Jerusalem, and to myriads of angels, to the general assembly and church of the firstborn who are enrolled in heaven, and to God, the Judge of all, and to the spirits of the righteous made perfect, and to Jesus, the mediator of a new covenant, and to the sprinkled blood, which speaks better than the blood of Abel" (Heb. 12:18-24).

## Jesus Christ Is the Same Yesterday and Today, and Forever

"Remember those who led you, who spoke the word of God to you; and considering the result of their conduct, imitate their faith. Jesus Christ is the same yesterday and today and forever. Do not be carried away by varied and strange teachings; for it is good for the heart to be strengthened by grace, not by foods, through which those who were so occupied were not benefited. We have an altar from which those who serve the tabernacle have no right to eat. For the bodies of those animals whose blood is brought into the holy place by the high priest as an offering for sin, are burned outside the camp. Therefore Jesus also, that He might sanctify the people through His own blood, suffered outside the gate. So, let us go out to Him outside the camp, bearing His reproach. For here we do not have a lasting city, but we are seeking the city which is to come. Through Him then, let us continually offer up a sacrifice of praise to God, that is, the fruit of lips that give thanks to His name. And do not neglect doing good and sharing, for with such sacrifices God is pleased" (Heb. 13:7-16).

## Jesus, the Great Shepherd of the Sheep

"Now the God of peace, who brought up from the dead the great Shepherd of the sheep through the blood of the eternal covenant, even Jesus our Lord, equip you in every good thing to do His will, working in us that which is pleasing in His sight, through Jesus Christ, to whom be the glory forever and ever. Amen" (Heb. 13:20-21).

## THE BOOK OF JAMES

## Our Glorious Lord Jesus Christ

"My brethren, do not hold your faith in our glorious Lord Jesus Christ with an attitude of personal favoritism. For if a man comes into your assembly with a gold ring and dressed in fine clothes, and there also comes in a poor man in dirty clothes, and you pay special attention to the one who is wearing the fine clothes, and say, 'You sit here in a good place," and you say to the poor man, "You stand over there, or sit down by my footstool,' have you not made distinctions among yourselves, and become judges with evil motives? Listen, my beloved brethren: did not God choose the poor of this world to be rich in faith and heirs of the kingdom which He promised to those who love Him? But you have dishonored the poor man. Is it not the rich who oppress you and personally drag you into court? Do they not blaspheme the fair name by which you have been called" (Jas. 2:1-7)?

*Chapter Three*

## THE BOOK OF 1 PETER

## Obey Jesus Christ and Be Sprinkled with His Blood

"Peter, an apostle of Jesus Christ, To those who reside as aliens, scattered throughout Pontus, Galatia, Cappadocia, Asia, and Bithynia, who are chosen according to the foreknowledge of God the Father, by the sanctifying work of the Spirit, to obey Jesus Christ and be sprinkled with His blood: May grace and peace be yours in the fullest measure" (1Pe. 1:1-2).

## Born Again to a Living Hope Through the Resurrection of Jesus

"Blessed be the God and Father of our Lord Jesus Christ, who according to His great mercy has caused us to be born again to a living hope through the resurrection of Jesus Christ from the dead, to obtain an inheritance which is imperishable and undefiled and will not fade away, reserved in heaven for you, who are protected by the power of God through faith for a salvation ready to be revealed in the last time. In this you greatly rejoice, even though now for a little while, if necessary, you have been distressed by various trials, so that the proof of your faith, being more precious than gold which is perishable, even though tested by fire, may be found to result in praise and glory and honor at the revelation of Jesus Christ; and though you have not seen Him, you love Him, and though you do not see Him now, but believe in Him, you greatly rejoice with joy inexpressible and full of glory, obtaining as the outcome of your faith the salvation of your souls" (1Pe. 1:3-9).

## The Revelation of Jesus Christ

"Therefore, prepare your minds for action, keep sober in spirit, fix your hope completely on the grace to be brought to you at the revelation of Jesus Christ. As obedient children, do not be conformed to the former lusts which were yours in your ignorance, but like the Holy One who called you, be holy yourselves also in all your behavior; because it is written, 'YOU SHALL BE HOLY, FOR I AM HOLY'" (1Pe. 1:13-16).

## Offer up Spiritual Sacrifices Acceptable to God Through Jesus Christ

"And coming to Him as to a living stone which has been rejected by men, but is choice and precious in the sight of God, you also, as living stones, are being built up as a spiritual house for a holy priesthood, to offer up spiritual sacrifices acceptable to God through Jesus Christ. For this is contained in Scripture: 'BEHOLD, I LAY IN ZION A CHOICE STONE, A PRECIOUS CORNER stone, AND HE WHO BELIEVES IN HIM WILL NOT BE DISAPPOINTED.' This precious value, then, is for you who believe; but for those who disbelieve, 'THE STONE WHICH THE BUILDERS REJECTED, THIS BECAME THE VERY CORNER stone,' and, 'A STONE OF STUMBLING AND A ROCK OF OFFENSE'; for they stumble because they are disobedient to the word, and to this doom they were also appointed" (1Pe. 2:4-8).

## The Resurrection of Jesus Christ

"Who is there to harm you if you prove zealous for what is good? But even if you should suffer for the sake of righteousness, you are blessed. AND DO NOT FEAR THEIR INTIMIDATION, AND DO NOT BE TROUBLED, but sanctify Christ as Lord in your hearts, always being ready to make a defense to everyone who asks you to give an account for the hope that is in you, yet with gentleness and reverence; and keep a good conscience so that in the thing in which you are slandered, those who revile your good behavior in Christ will be put to shame. For it is better, if God should will it so, that you suffer for doing what is right rather than for doing what is wrong. For Christ also died for sins once for all, the just for the unjust, so that He might bring us to God, having been put to death in the flesh, but made alive in the spirit; in which also He went and made proclamation to the spirits now in prison, who once were disobedient, when the patience of God kept waiting in the days of Noah, during the construction of the ark, in which a few, that is, eight persons, were brought safely through the water. Corresponding to that, baptism now saves you—not the removal of dirt from the flesh, but an appeal to God for a good conscience—through the resurrection of Jesus Christ, who is at the right hand of God, having gone into heaven, after angels and authorities and powers had been subjected to Him" (1Pe. 3:13-22).

## So that in All Things God May Be Glorified Through Jesus Christ

"The end of all things is near; therefore, be of sound judgment and sober spirit for the purpose of prayer. Above all, keep fervent in your love for one another, because love covers a multitude of sins. Be hospitable to one another without complaint. As each one has received a special gift, employ it in serving one another as good stewards of the manifold grace of God. Whoever speaks, is to do so as one who is speaking the utterances of God; whoever serves is to do so as one who is serving by the strength which God supplies; so that in all things God may be glorified through Jesus Christ, to whom belongs the glory and dominion forever and ever. Amen" (1Pe. 4:7-11).

## THE BOOK OF 2 PETER

## The True Knowledge of Our Lord Jesus Christ

"Simon Peter, a bond-servant and apostle of Jesus Christ, To those who have received a faith of the same kind as ours, by the righteousness of our God and Savior, Jesus Christ: Grace and peace be multiplied to you in the knowledge of God and of Jesus our Lord; seeing that His divine power has granted to us everything pertaining to life and godliness, through the true knowledge of Him who called us by His own glory and excellence. For by these He has granted to us His precious and magnificent promises, so that by them you may become partakers of the divine nature, having escaped the corruption that is in the world by lust. Now for this very reason also, applying all diligence, in your faith supply moral excellence, and in your moral excellence, knowledge, and in your knowledge, self-control, and in your self-control, perseverance, and in your perseverance, godliness, and in your godliness, brotherly kindness, and in your brotherly kindness, love. For if these qualities are yours and are increasing, they render you neither useless nor unfruitful in the true knowledge of our Lord Jesus Christ. For he who lacks these qualities is blind or short-sighted, having forgotten his purification from his former sins. Therefore, brethren, be all the more diligent to make certain about His calling and choosing you; for as long as you practice these things, you will never stumble; for in this way the entrance into the eternal kingdom of our Lord and Savior Jesus Christ will be abundantly supplied to you" (2Pe. 1:1-11).

## Our Lord Jesus Christ Has Made Clear to Me

"Therefore, I will always be ready to remind you of these things, even though you already know them, and have been established in the truth which is present with you. I consider it right, as long as I am in this earthly dwelling, to stir you up by way of reminder, knowing that the laying aside of my earthly dwelling is imminent, as also our Lord Jesus Christ has made clear to me. And I will also be diligent that at any time after my departure you will be able to call these things to mind" (2Pe. 1:12-15).

*Chapter Three*

**The Power and Coming of Our Lord Jesus Christ**

"For we did not follow cleverly devised tales when we made known to you the power and coming of our Lord Jesus Christ, but we were eyewitnesses of His majesty. For when He received honor and glory from God the Father, such an utterance as this was made to Him by the Majestic Glory, 'This is My beloved Son with whom I am well-pleased'—and we ourselves heard this utterance made from heaven when we were with Him on the holy mountain" (2Pe. 1:16-18).

**They Escaped by the Knowledge of Jesus**

"These are springs without water and mists driven by a storm, for whom the black darkness has been reserved. For speaking out arrogant words of vanity they entice by fleshly desires, by sensuality, those who barely escape from the ones who live in error, promising them freedom while they themselves are slaves of corruption; for by what a man is overcome, by this he is enslaved. For if, after they have escaped the defilements of the world by the knowledge of the Lord and Savior Jesus Christ, they are again entangled in them and are overcome, the last state has become worse for them than the first. For it would be better for them not to have known the way of righteousness, than having known it, to turn away from the holy commandment handed on to them. It has happened to them according to the true proverb, 'A DOG RETURNS TO ITS OWN VOMIT,' and, 'A sow, after washing, returns to wallowing in the mire'" (2Pe. 2:17-22).

*Chapter Three*

## Grow in the Grace and Knowledge of Jesus

"Therefore, beloved, since you look for these things, be diligent to be found by Him in peace, spotless and blameless, and regard the patience of our Lord as salvation; just as also our beloved brother Paul, according to the wisdom given him, wrote to you, as also in all his letters, speaking in them of these things, in which are some things hard to understand, which the untaught and unstable distort, as they do also the rest of the Scriptures, to their own destruction. You therefore, beloved, knowing this beforehand, be on your guard so that you are not carried away by the error of unprincipled men and fall from your own steadfastness, but grow in the grace and knowledge of our Lord and Savior Jesus Christ. To Him be the glory, both now and to the day of eternity. Amen" (2Pe. 3:14-18).

## THE BOOK OF 1 JOHN

## Our Fellowship Is with the Father, and Jesus

"What was from the beginning, what we have heard, what we have seen with our eyes, what we have looked at and touched with our hands, concerning the Word of Life—and the life was manifested, and we have seen and testify and proclaim to you the eternal life, which was with the Father and was manifested to us—what we have seen and heard we proclaim to you also, so that you too may have fellowship with us; and indeed our fellowship is with the Father, and with His Son Jesus

Christ. These things we write, so that our joy may be made complete" (1Jn. 1:1-4).

## The Blood of Jesus His Son Cleanses Us

"This is the message we have heard from Him and announce to you, that God is Light, and in Him there is no darkness at all. If we say that we have fellowship with Him and yet walk in the darkness, we lie and do not practice the truth; but if we walk in the Light as He Himself is in the Light, we have fellowship with one another, and the blood of Jesus His Son cleanses us from all sin. If we say that we have no sin, we are deceiving ourselves and the truth is not in us. If we confess our sins, He is faithful and righteous to forgive us our sins and to cleanse us from all unrighteousness. If we say that we have not sinned, we make Him a liar and His word is not in us" (1Jn. 1:5-10).

## Jesus Our Advocate

"My little children, I am writing these things to you so that you may not sin. And if anyone sins, we have an Advocate with the Father, Jesus Christ the righteous; and He Himself is the propitiation for our sins; and not for ours only, but also for those of the whole world" (1Jn. 2:1-2).

## The Liar Denies that Jesus Is the Christ

"Children, it is the last hour; and just as you heard that antichrist is coming, even now many antichrists have appeared; from this we know that it is the last hour. They went out from us, but they were not really of us; for if they had been of us, they would have remained with us; but they went out, so that it would be shown that they all are not of us. But you have an anointing from the Holy One, and you all know. I have not written to you because you do not know the truth, but because you do know it, and because no lie is of the truth. Who is the liar but the one who denies that Jesus is the Christ? This is the antichrist, the one who denies the Father and the Son. Whoever denies the Son does not have the Father; the one who confesses the Son has the Father also. As for you, let that abide in you which you heard from the beginning. If what you heard from the beginning abides in you, you also will abide in the Son and in the Father. This is the promise which He Himself made to us: eternal life" (1Jn. 2:18-25).

## We Believe in the Name Jesus

"This is His commandment, that we believe in the name of His Son Jesus Christ, and love one another, just as He commanded us. The one who keeps His commandments abides in Him, and He in him. We know by this that He abides in us, by the Spirit whom He has given us" (1Jn. 3:23-24).

## Jesus Christ Has Come in the Flesh

"Beloved, do not believe every spirit, but test the spirits to see whether they are from God, because many false prophets have gone out into the world. By this you know the Spirit of God: every spirit that confesses that Jesus Christ has come in the flesh is from God; and every spirit that does not confess Jesus is not from God; this is the spirit of the antichrist, of which you have heard that it is coming, and now it is already in the world. You are from God, little children, and have overcome them; because greater is He who is in you than he who is in the world. They are from the world; therefore they speak as from the world, and the world listens to them. We are from God; he who knows God listens to us; he who is not from God does not listen to us. By this we know the spirit of truth and the spirit of error" (1Jn. 4:1-6).

## Jesus Is the Son of God

"Whoever confesses that Jesus is the Son of God, God abides in him, and he in God. We have come to know and have believed the love which God has for us. God is love, and the one who abides in love abides in God, and God abides in him. By this, love is perfected with us, so that we may have confidence in the Day of Judgment; because as He is, so also are we in this world. There is no fear in love; but perfect love casts out fear, because fear involves punishment, and the one who fears is not perfected in love. We love, because He first loved us. If someone says, 'I love God,' and hates his brother, he is a liar; for the one who does not love his brother whom he has seen, cannot love God whom he has not seen. And this commandment we have from Him, that the one who loves God should love his brother also" (1Jn. 4:15-21).

*Chapter Three*

## Jesus Is the Christ

"Whoever believes that Jesus is the Christ is born of God, and whoever loves the Father loves the child born of Him. By this we know that we love the children of God, when we love God and observe His commandments. For this is the love of God, that we keep His commandments; and His commandments are not burdensome. For whatever is born of God overcomes the world; and this is the victory that has overcome the world—our faith" (1Jn. 5:1-4).

## He Who Believes that Jesus Is the Son of God

"Who is the one who overcomes the world, but he who believes that Jesus is the Son of God? This is the One who came by water and blood, Jesus Christ; not with the water only, but with the water and with the blood. It is the Spirit who testifies, because the Spirit is the truth. For there are three that testify: the Spirit and the water and the blood; and the three are in agreement. If we receive the testimony of men, the testimony of God is greater; for the testimony of God is this, that He has testified concerning His Son. The one who believes in the Son of God has the testimony in himself; the one who does not believe God has made Him a liar, because he has not believed in the testimony that God has given concerning His Son. And the testimony is this, that God has given us eternal life, and this life is in His Son. He who has the Son has the life; he who does not have the Son of God does not have the life" (1Jn. 5:5-12).

*Chapter Three*

## In His Son Jesus Christ

"We know that no one who is born of God sins; but He who was born of God keeps him, and the evil one does not touch him. We know that we are of God, and that the whole world lies in the power of the evil one. And we know that the Son of God has come, and has given us understanding so that we may know Him who is true; and we are in Him who is true, in His Son Jesus Christ. This is the true God and eternal life" (1Jn. 5:18-20).

## THE BOOK OF 2 JOHN

## Grace, Mercy and Peace from the Father and Jesus

"The elder to the chosen lady and her children, whom I love in truth; and not only I, but also all who know the truth, for the sake of the truth which abides in us and will be with us forever: Grace, mercy and peace will be with us, from God the Father and from Jesus Christ, the Son of the Father, in truth and love" (2Jn. 1:1-3).

## Who Do Not Acknowledge Jesus as Coming in the Flesh

"For many deceivers have gone out into the world, those who do not acknowledge Jesus Christ as coming in the flesh. This is the deceiver and the antichrist. Watch yourselves, that you do not lose what we have accomplished, but that you may receive a full reward. Anyone who goes too far and does not abide in the teaching of Christ, does not have God; the one who abides in the teaching, he has both the Father and the Son. If anyone comes to you and does not bring this teaching, do not receive him into your house, and do not give him a greeting; for the one who gives him a greeting participates in his evil deeds" (2Jn. 1:7-11).

## THE BOOK OF JUDE

### Kept for Jesus

"Jude, a bond-servant of Jesus Christ, and brother of James, To those who are the called, beloved in God the Father, and kept for Jesus Christ: May mercy and peace and love be multiplied to you" (Jude 1:1-2).

### Deny Our Only Master and Lord, Jesus Christ

"Beloved, while I was making every effort to write you about our common salvation, I felt the necessity to write to you appealing that you contend earnestly for the faith which was once for all handed down to the saints. For certain persons have crept in unnoticed, those who were long beforehand marked out for this condemnation, ungodly persons who turn the grace of our God into licentiousness and deny our only Master and Lord, Jesus Christ" (Jude 1:3-4).

*Chapter Three*

## Spoken Beforehand by the Apostles of Our Lord Jesus Christ

"But you, beloved, ought to remember the words that were spoken beforehand by the apostles of our Lord Jesus Christ, that they were saying to you, 'In the last time there will be mockers, following after their own ungodly lusts.' These are the ones who cause divisions, worldly-minded, devoid of the Spirit. But you, beloved, building yourselves up on your most holy faith, praying in the Holy Spirit, keep yourselves in the love of God, waiting anxiously for the mercy of our Lord Jesus Christ to eternal life. And have mercy on some, who are doubting; save others, snatching them out of the fire; and on some have mercy with fear, hating even the garment polluted by the flesh" (Jude 1:17-23).

## Through Jesus Christ Our Lord, Be Glory, Majesty, Dominion and Authority

"Now to Him who is able to keep you from stumbling, and to make you stand in the presence of His glory blameless with great joy, to the only God our Savior, through Jesus Christ our Lord, be glory, majesty, dominion and authority, before all time and now and forever. Amen" (Jude 1:24-25).

# AUTHORITY IN THE NEW TESTAMENT

## IN THE BOOK OF MATTHEW

### He was Teaching Them as One Having Authority

"When Jesus had finished these words, the crowds were amazed at His teaching; for He was teaching them as one having authority, and not as their scribes" (Mt. 7:28-29).

### I Also Am a Man Under Authority

"And when Jesus entered Capernaum, a centurion came to Him, imploring Him, and saying, 'Lord, my servant is lying paralyzed at home, fearfully tormented.' Jesus said to him, 'I will come and heal him.' But the centurion said, 'Lord, I am not worthy for You to come under my roof, but just say the word, and my servant will be healed. For I also am a man under authority, with soldiers under me; and I say to this one, "Go!" and he goes, and to another, "Come!" and he comes, and to my slave, "Do this!" and he does it.' Now when Jesus heard this, He marveled and said to those who were following, 'Truly I say to you, I have not found such great faith with anyone in Israel. "I say to you that many will come from east and west, and recline at the table with Abraham, Isaac and Jacob in the kingdom of heaven; but the sons of the kingdom will be cast out into the outer darkness; in that place there will be weeping and gnashing of teeth.' And

Jesus said to the centurion, 'Go; it shall be done for you as you have believed.' And the servant was healed that very moment" (Mt. 8:5-13).

## The Son of Man Has Authority on Earth to Forgive Sins

"And they brought to Him a paralytic lying on a bed. Seeing their faith, Jesus said to the paralytic, 'Take courage, son; your sins are forgiven.' And some of the scribes said to themselves, 'This fellow blasphemes.' And Jesus knowing their thoughts said, 'Why are you thinking evil in your hearts? Which is easier, to say, "Your sins are forgiven," or to say, "Get up, and walk"? But so that you may know that the Son of Man has authority on earth to forgive sins" — then He said to the paralytic, 'Get up, pick up your bed and go home.' And he got up and went home. But when the crowds saw this, they were awestruck, and glorified God, who had given such authority to men" (Mt. 9:2-8).

## His Twelve Disciples and Gave Them Authority Over Unclean Spirits

"Jesus summoned His twelve disciples and gave them authority over unclean spirits, to cast them out, and to heal every kind of disease and every kind of sickness" (Mt. 10:1).

## Their Great Men Exercise Authority over Them

"And hearing this, the ten became indignant with the two brothers. But Jesus called them to

Himself and said, 'You know that the rulers of the Gentiles lord it over them, and their great men exercise authority over them. It is not this way among you, but whoever wishes to become great among you shall be your servant, and whoever wishes to be first among you shall be your slave; just as the Son of Man did not come to be served, but to serve, and to give His life a ransom for many'" (Mt. 20:24-28).

## By What Authority Are You Doing These Things

"When He entered the temple, the chief priests and the elders of the people came to Him while He was teaching, and said, 'By what authority are You doing these things, and who gave You this authority?' Jesus said to them, 'I will also ask you one thing, which if you tell Me, I will also tell you by what authority I do these things. The baptism of John was from what source, from heaven or from men?' And they began reasoning among themselves, saying, 'If we say, "From heaven," He will say to us, "Then why did you not believe him?" But if we say, "From men," we fear the people; for they all regard John as a prophet.' And answering Jesus, they said, 'We do not know.' He also said to them, "Neither will I tell you by what authority I do these things'" (Mt. 21:23-27).

## All Authority Has Been Given to Me

"But the eleven disciples proceeded to Galilee, to the mountain which Jesus had designated. When they saw Him, they worshiped Him; but some were doubtful. And Jesus came up and spoke to them, saying, 'All authority has been given to Me in heaven and on earth. Go therefore and make disciples of all the nations, baptizing them in the name of the Father and the Son and the Holy Spirit, teaching them to observe all that I commanded you; and lo, I am with you always, even to the end of the age'" (Mt. 28:16-20).

## IN THE BOOK OF MARK

### He Was Teaching Them as One Having Authority

"They went into Capernaum; and immediately on the Sabbath He entered the synagogue and began to teach. They were amazed at His teaching; for He was teaching them as one having authority, and not as the scribes. Just then there was a man in their synagogue with an unclean spirit; and he cried out, saying, 'What business do we have with each other, Jesus of Nazareth? Have You come to destroy us? I know who You are—the Holy One of God!' And Jesus rebuked him, saying, 'Be quiet, and come out of him!' Throwing him into convulsions, the unclean spirit cried out with a loud voice and came out of him. They were all amazed, so that they debated among themselves, saying, 'What is this? A new teaching with authority! He commands even the unclean spirits, and they obey Him.' Immediately the news about Him spread everywhere into all the surrounding district of Galilee" (Mk. 1:21-28).

*Chapter Four*

## The Son of Man has Authority on Earth

"When He had come back to Capernaum several days afterward, it was heard that He was at home. And many were gathered together, so that there was no longer room, not even near the door; and He was speaking the word to them. And they came, bringing to Him a paralytic, carried by four men. Being unable to get to Him because of the crowd, they removed the roof above Him; and when they had dug an opening, they let down the pallet on which the paralytic was lying. And Jesus seeing their faith said to the paralytic, 'Son, your sins are forgiven.' But some of the scribes were sitting there and reasoning in their hearts, 'Why does this man speak that way? He is blaspheming; who can forgive sins but God alone?' Immediately Jesus, aware in His spirit that they were reasoning that way within themselves, said to them, 'Why are you reasoning about these things in your hearts? Which is easier, to say to the paralytic, "Your sins are forgiven"; or to say, "Get up, and pick up your pallet and walk"? But so that you may know that the Son of Man has authority on earth to forgive sins'—He said to the paralytic, 'I say to you, get up, pick up your pallet and go home.' And he got up and immediately picked up the pallet and went out in the sight of everyone, so that they were all amazed and were glorifying God, saying, 'We have never seen anything like this'" (Mk. 2:1-12).

## To Have Authority to Cast out the Demons

"And He went up on the mountain and summoned those whom He Himself wanted, and they came to Him. And He appointed twelve, so that they would be with Him and that He could send them out to preach, and to have authority to cast out the demons. And He appointed the twelve: Simon (to whom He gave the name Peter), and James, the son of Zebedee, and John the brother of James (to them He gave the name Boanerges, which means, 'Sons of Thunder'); and Andrew, and Philip, and Bartholomew, and Matthew, and Thomas, and James the son of Alphaeus, and Thaddaeus, and Simon the Zealot; and Judas Iscariot, who betrayed Him" (Mk. 3:13-19).

## And Gave Them Authority over the Unclean Spirits

"And He summoned the twelve and began to send them out in pairs, and gave them authority over the unclean spirits; and He instructed them that they should take nothing for their journey, except a mere staff—no bread, no bag, no money in their belt—but to wear sandals; and He added, 'Do not put on two tunics.' And He said to them, 'Wherever you enter a house, stay there until you leave town. Any place that does not receive you or listen to you, as you go out from there, shake the dust off the soles of your feet for a testimony against them.' They went out and preached that men should repent. And they were casting out many demons and were anointing with oil many sick people and healing them" (Mk.

6:7-13).

## Their Great Men Exercise Authority over Them

"Hearing this, the ten began to feel indignant with James and John. Calling them to Himself, Jesus said to them, 'You know that those who are recognized as rulers of the Gentiles lord it over them; and their great men exercise authority over them. But it is not this way among you, but whoever wishes to become great among you shall be your servant; and whoever wishes to be first among you shall be slave of all. For even the Son of Man did not come to be served, but to serve, and to give His life a ransom for many'" (Mk. 10:41-45).

## Who Gave You this Authority

"They came again to Jerusalem. And as He was walking in the temple, the chief priests and the scribes and the elders came to Him, and began saying to Him, 'By what authority are You doing these things, or who gave You this authority to do these things?' And Jesus said to them, 'I will ask you one question, and you answer Me, and then I will tell you by what authority I do these things. Was the baptism of John from heaven, or from men? Answer Me.' They began reasoning among themselves, saying, 'If we say, "From heaven," He will say, "Then why did you not believe him?" But shall we say, "From men"?' — they were afraid of the people, for everyone considered John to have been a real prophet. Answering Jesus, they said, 'We do not know.' And Jesus said to them, 'Nor will I tell you by what authority I do these things'" (Mk. 11:27-33).

## IN THE BOOK OF LUKE

### His Message Was with Authority

"And He came down to Capernaum, a city of Galilee, and He was teaching them on the Sabbath; and they were amazed at His teaching, for His message was with authority. In the synagogue there was a man possessed by the spirit of an unclean demon, and he cried out with a loud voice, 'Let us alone! What business do we have with each other, Jesus of Nazareth? Have You come to destroy us? I know who You are—the Holy One of God!' But Jesus rebuked him, saying, 'Be quiet and come out of him!' And when the demon had thrown him down in the midst of the people, he came out of him without doing him any harm. And amazement came upon them all, and they began talking with one another saying, 'What is this message? For with authority and power He commands the unclean spirits and they come out.' And the report about Him was spreading into every locality in the surrounding district" (Lk. 4:31-37).

### The Son of Man Has Authority on Earth

"One day He was teaching; and there were some Pharisees and teachers of the law sitting there, who had come from every village of Galilee and Judea and from Jerusalem; and the power of the Lord was present for Him to perform healing. And some men were carrying on a bed a man who was paralyzed; and they were trying to bring him in and to set him down in front of Him. But not finding any way to bring him in because of the crowd, they went up on the roof and let him down through the tiles with his stretcher, into the middle of the crowd, in front of Jesus. Seeing their faith, He said, 'Friend, your sins are forgiven you.' The scribes and the Pharisees began to reason, saying, 'Who is this man who speaks blasphemies? Who can forgive sins, but God alone?' But Jesus, aware of their reasonings, answered and said to them, 'Why are you reasoning in your hearts? Which is easier, to say, "Your sins have been forgiven you," or to say, "Get up and walk"? But, so that you may know that the Son of Man has authority on earth to forgive sins,'—He said to the paralytic—'I say to you, get up, and pick up your stretcher and go home.' Immediately he got up before them, and picked up what he had been lying on, and went home glorifying God. They were all struck with astonishment and began glorifying God; and they were filled with fear, saying, 'We have seen remarkable things today'" (Lk. 5:17-26).

## Placed Under Authority, with Soldiers Under Me

"When He had completed all His discourse in the hearing of the people, He went to Capernaum. And a centurion's slave, who was highly regarded by him, was sick and about to die. When he heard about Jesus, he sent some Jewish elders asking Him to come and save the life of his slave. When they came to Jesus, they earnestly implored Him, saying, 'He is worthy for You to grant this to him; for he loves our nation and it was he who built us our synagogue." Now Jesus started on His way with them; and when He was not far from the house, the centurion sent friends, saying to Him, 'Lord, do not trouble Yourself further, for I am not worthy for You to come under my roof; for this reason I did not even consider myself worthy to come to You, but just say the word, and my servant will be healed. For I also am a man placed under authority, with soldiers under me; and I say to this one, "Go!" and he goes, and to another, "Come!" and he comes, and to my slave, "Do this!" and he does it.' Now when Jesus heard this, He marveled at him, and turned and said to the crowd that was following Him, 'I say to you, not even in Israel have I found such great faith.' When those who had been sent returned to the house, they found the slave in good health" (Lk. 7:1-10).

## Gave them Power and Authority over All the Demons

"And He called the twelve together, and gave them power and authority over all the demons and to heal diseases. And He sent them out to proclaim the kingdom of God and to perform healing. And He said to them, 'Take nothing for your journey, neither a staff, nor a bag, nor bread, nor money; and do not even have two tunics apiece. Whatever house you enter, stay there until you leave that city. And as for those who do not receive you, as you go out from that city, shake the dust off your feet as a testimony against them.' Departing, they began going throughout the villages, preaching the gospel and healing everywhere" (Lk. 9:1-6).

# Given You Authority to Tread on Serpents and Scorpions

"The seventy returned with joy, saying, 'Lord, even the demons are subject to us in Your name.' And He said to them, 'I was watching Satan fall from heaven like lightning. Behold, I have given you authority to tread on serpents and scorpions, and over all the power of the enemy, and nothing will injure you. Nevertheless do not rejoice in this, that the spirits are subject to you, but rejoice that your names are recorded in heaven'" (Lk. 10:17-20).

## He Has Authority to Cast into Hell

"I say to you, My friends, do not be afraid of those who kill the body and after that have no more that they can do. But I will warn you whom to fear: fear the One who, after He has killed, has authority to cast into hell; yes, I tell you, fear Him! Are not five sparrows sold for two cents? Yet not one of them is forgotten before God. Indeed, the very hairs of your head are all numbered. Do not fear; you are more valuable than many sparrows" (Lk. 12:4-7).

## You Are to Be in Authority over Ten Cities

"While they were listening to these things, Jesus went on to tell a parable, because He was near Jerusalem, and they supposed that the kingdom of God was going to appear immediately. So He said, 'A nobleman went to a distant country to receive a kingdom for himself, and then return. And he called ten of his slaves, and gave them ten minas and said to them, "Do business with this until I come back." But his citizens hated him and sent a delegation after him, saying, "We do not want this man to reign over us." When he returned, after receiving the kingdom, he ordered that these slaves, to whom he had given the money, be called to him so that he might know what business they had done. The first appeared, saying, "Master, your mina has made ten minas more." And he said to him, "Well done, good slave, because you have been faithful in a very little thing, you are to be in authority over ten cities." The second came, saying, 'Your mina, master, has made five minas." And he said to him also, "And you are to be over five cities." Another came, saying, "Master, here is your mina, which I kept put away in a handkerchief; for I was afraid of you, because you are an exacting man; you take up what you did not lay down and reap what you did not sow." He said to him, "By your own words I will judge you, you worthless slave. Did you know that I am an exacting man, taking up what I did not lay down and reaping what I did not sow? Then why did you not put my money in the bank, and having come, I would have collected it with interest?" Then he said to the bystanders, "Take the mina away from him and give it to the one who has the ten minas." And they said to him, "Master, he has ten minas already." I tell you that to everyone who has, more shall be given, but from the one who does not have, even what he does have shall be taken away. But these enemies of mine, who did not want me to reign over them, bring them here and slay them in my presence'" (Lk. 19:11-27).

*Chapter Four*

## Who Is the One Who Gave You this Authority?

"On one of the days while He was teaching the people in the temple and preaching the gospel, the chief priests and the scribes with the elders confronted Him,  and they spoke, saying to Him, 'Tell us by what authority You are doing these things, or who is the one who gave You this authority?' Jesus answered and said to them, 'I will also ask you a question, and you tell Me: "Was the baptism of John from heaven or from men?" They reasoned among themselves, saying, 'If we say, "From heaven," He will say, "Why did you not believe him?" But if we say, "From men," all the people will stone us to death, for they are convinced that John was a prophet.' So they answered that they did not know where it came from. And Jesus said to them, 'Nor will I tell you by what authority I do these things'" (Lk. 20:1-8).

## The Rule and the Authority of the Governor

"The scribes and the chief priests tried to lay hands on Him that very hour, and they feared the people; for they understood that He spoke this parable against them.  So they watched Him, and sent spies who pretended to be righteous, in order that they might catch Him in some statement, so that they could deliver Him to the rule and the authority of the governor. They questioned Him, saying, 'Teacher, we know that You speak and teach correctly, and You are not partial to any, but teach the way of God in truth. Is it lawful for us to pay taxes to Caesar, or not?' But He detected their trickery and said to them, 'Show Me a denarius. Whose likeness and inscription does it have?' They said, 'Caesar's.' And He said to them, 'Then render to Caesar the things that are Caesar's, and to God the things that are God's.' And they were unable to catch Him in a saying in the presence of the people; and being amazed at His answer, they became silent" (Lk. 20:19-26).

## And Those Who Have Authority over Them

"And there arose also a dispute among them as to which one of them was regarded to be greatest. And He said to them, 'The kings of the Gentiles lord it over them; and those who have authority over them are called "Benefactors." But it is not this way with you, but the one who is the greatest among you must become like the youngest, and the leader like the servant. For who is greater, the one who reclines at the table or the one who serves? Is it not the one who reclines at the table? But I am among you as the one who serves'" (Lk. 22:24-27).

## IN THE BOOK OF JOHN

## What Sign Do You Show Us as Your Authority

"The Passover of the Jews was near, and Jesus went up to Jerusalem. And He found in the temple those who were selling oxen and sheep and doves, and the money changers seated at their tables. And He made a scourge of cords, and drove them all out of the temple, with the sheep and the oxen; and He poured out the coins of the money changers and overturned their tables; and to those who were selling the doves He said, 'Take these things away; stop making My Father's house a place of business.' His disciples remembered that it was written, 'ZEAL FOR YOUR HOUSE WILL CONSUME ME.' The Jews then said to Him, 'What sign do You show us as your authority for doing these things?' Jesus answered them, 'Destroy this temple, and in three days I will raise it up.' The Jews then said, 'It took forty-six years to build this temple, and will You raise it up in three days?' But He was speaking of the temple of His body. So when He was raised from the dead, His disciples remembered that He said this; and they believed the Scripture and the word which Jesus had spoken. Now when He was in Jerusalem at the Passover, during the feast, many believed in His name, observing His signs which He was doing. But Jesus, on His part, was not entrusting Himself to them, for He knew all men, and because He did not need anyone to testify concerning man, for He Himself knew what was in man" (Jn. 2:13-25).

## He Gave Him Authority to Execute Judgment

"Truly, truly, I say to you, he who hears My word, and believes Him who sent Me, has eternal life, and does not come into judgment, but has passed out of death into life. Truly, truly, I say to you, an hour is coming and now is, when the dead shall hear the voice of the Son of God; and those who hear shall live. For just as the Father has life in Himself, even so He gave to the Son also to have life in Himself; and He gave Him authority to execute judgment, because He is the Son of Man. Do not marvel at this; for an hour is coming, in which all who are in the tombs shall hear His voice, and shall come forth; those who did the good deeds to a resurrection of life, those who committed the evil deeds to a resurrection of judgment" (Jn. 5:24-29).

## I Have Authority to Lay it Down, and I Have Authority to Take it Up Again

"I am the good shepherd; the good shepherd lays down His life for the sheep. He who is a hireling, and not a shepherd, who is not the owner of the sheep, beholds the wolf coming, and leaves the sheep, and flees, and the wolf snatches them, and scatters them. He flees because he is a hireling, and is not concerned about the sheep. I am the good shepherd; and I know My own, and My own know Me, even as the Father knows Me and I know the Father; and I lay down My life for the sheep. And I have other sheep, which are not of this fold; I must bring them also, and they shall hear My voice; and they shall become one flock with one shepherd. For this reason the Father loves Me, because I lay down My life that I may take it again. No one has taken it away from Me, but I lay it down on My own initiative. I have authority to lay it down, and I have authority to take it up again. This commandment I received from My Father" (Jn. 10:11-18).

## You Gave Him Authority over All Flesh

"These things Jesus spoke; and lifting up His eyes to heaven, He said, 'Father, the hour has come; glorify Thy Son, that the Son may glorify Thee, even as Thou gavest Him authority over all mankind, that to all whom Thou hast given Him, He may give eternal life. And this is eternal life, that they may know Thee, the only true God, and Jesus Christ whom Thou hast sent. I glorified Thee on the earth, having accomplished the work which Thou hast given Me to do. And now, glorify Thou Me together with Thyself, Father, with the glory which I had with Thee before the world was'" (Jn. 17:1-5).

## I Have Authority to Release You

"When Pilate therefore heard this statement, he was the more afraid; and he entered into the Praetorium again, and said to Jesus, 'Where are You from?' But Jesus gave him no answer. Pilate therefore said to Him, 'You do not speak to me? Do You not know that I have authority to release You, and I have authority to crucify You?' Jesus answered, 'You would have no authority over Me, unless it had been given you from above; for this reason he who delivered Me up to you has the greater sin.' As a result of this Pilate made efforts to release Him, but the Jews cried out, saying, 'If you release this Man, you are no friend of Caesar; everyone who makes himself out to be a king opposes Caesar'" (Jn. 19:8-12).

## IN THE BOOK OF ACTS

## The Father Has Fixed by His Own Authority

"And so when they had come together, they were asking Him, saying, 'Lord, is it at this time You are restoring the kingdom to Israel?' He said to them, 'It is not for you to know times or epochs which the Father has fixed by His own authority; but you shall receive power when the Holy Spirit has come upon you; and you shall be My witnesses both in Jerusalem, and in all Judea and Samaria, and even to the remotest part of the earth.' And after He had said these things, He was lifted up while they were looking on, and a cloud received Him out of their sight. And as they were gazing intently into the sky while He was departing, behold, two men in white clothing stood beside them; and they also said, 'Men of Galilee, why do you stand looking into the sky? This Jesus, who has been taken up from you into heaven, will come in just the same way as you have watched Him go into heaven'" (Ac. 1:6-11).

## Give this Authority to Me as Well

"Now when the apostles in Jerusalem heard that Samaria had received the word of God, they sent them Peter and John, who came down and prayed for them, that they might receive the Holy Spirit. For He had not yet fallen upon any of them; they had simply been baptized in the name of the Lord Jesus. Then they began laying their hands on them, and they were receiving the Holy Spirit. Now when Simon saw that the Spirit was bestowed through the laying on of the apostles' hands, he offered them money, saying, 'Give this authority to me as well, so that everyone on whom I lay my hands may receive the Holy Spirit.' But Peter said to him, 'May your silver perish with you, because you thought you could obtain the gift of God with money! You have no part or portion in this matter, for your heart is not right before God. Therefore repent of this wickedness of yours, and pray the Lord that if possible, the intention of your heart may be forgiven you. For I see that you are in the gall of bitterness and in the bondage of iniquity.' But Simon answered and said, 'Pray to the Lord for me yourselves, so that nothing of what you have said may come upon me'" (Ac. 8:14-24).

## He Has Authority from the Chief Priests

"Now there was a certain disciple at Damascus, named Ananias; and the Lord said to him in a vision, 'Ananias.' And he said, 'Behold, here am I, Lord.' And the Lord said to him, 'Arise and go to the street called Straight, and inquire at the house of Judas for a man from Tarsus named Saul, for behold, he is praying, and he has seen in a vision a man named Ananias come in and lay his hands on him, so that he might regain his sight.' But Ananias answered, 'Lord, I have heard from many about this man, how much harm he did to Thy saints at Jerusalem; and here he has authority from the chief priests to bind all who call upon Thy name.' But the Lord said to him, 'Go, for he is a chosen instrument of Mine, to bear My name before the Gentiles and kings and the sons of Israel; for I will show him how much he must suffer for My name's sake.' And Ananias departed and entered the house, and after laying his hands on him said, 'Brother Saul, the Lord Jesus, who appeared to you on the road by which you were coming, has sent me so that you may regain your sight, and be filled with the Holy Spirit.'

And immediately there fell from his eyes something like scales, and he regained his sight, and he arose and was baptized; and he took food and was strengthened. Now for several days he was with the disciples who were at Damascus, and immediately he began to proclaim Jesus in the synagogues, saying, 'He is the Son of God.' And all those hearing him continued to be amazed, and were saying, 'Is this not he who in Jerusalem destroyed those who called on this name, and who had come here for the purpose of bringing them bound before the chief priests?' But Saul kept increasing in strength and confounding the Jews who lived at Damascus by proving that this Jesus is the Christ." (Ac. 9:10-22).

## Received Authority

"So then, I thought to myself that I had to do many things hostile to the name of Jesus of Nazareth. And this is just what I did in Jerusalem; not only did I lock up many of the saints in prisons, having received authority from the chief priests, but also when they were being put to death I cast my vote against them. And as I punished them often in all the synagogues, I tried to force them to blaspheme; and being furiously enraged at them, I kept pursuing them even to foreign cities" (Ac. 26:9-11).

## With the Authority and Commission of the Chief Priests

"While thus engaged as I was journeying to Damascus with the authority and commission of the chief priests, at midday, O King, I saw on the way a light from heaven, brighter than the sun, shining all around me and those who were journeying with me. And when we had all fallen to the ground, I heard a voice saying to me in the Hebrew dialect, 'Saul, Saul, why are you persecuting Me? It is hard for you to kick against the goads.' And I said, 'Who art Thou, Lord?' And the Lord said, 'I am Jesus whom you are persecuting. But arise, and stand on your feet; for this purpose I have appeared to you, to appoint you a minister and a witness not only to the things which you have seen, but also to the things in which I will appear to you; delivering you from the Jewish people and from the Gentiles, to whom I am sending you, to open their eyes so that they may turn from darkness to light and from the dominion of Satan to God, in order that they may receive forgiveness of sins and an inheritance among those who have been sanctified by faith in Me.' (Ac. 26:12-18).

## IN THE BOOK OF ROMANS

### There Is No Authority Except from God

"Let every person be in subjection to the governing authorities. For there is no authority except from God, and those which exist are established by God. Therefore he who resists authority has opposed the ordinance of God; and they who have opposed will receive condemnation upon themselves. For rulers are not a cause of fear for good behavior, but for evil. Do you want to have no fear of authority? Do what is good, and you will have praise from the same; for it is a minister of God to you for good. But if you do what is evil, be afraid; for it does not bear the sword for nothing; for it is a minister of God, an avenger who brings wrath upon the one who practices evil. Wherefore it is necessary to be in subjection, not only because of wrath, but also for conscience' sake. For because of this you also pay taxes, for rulers are servants of God, devoting themselves to this very thing. Render to all what is due them: tax to whom tax is due; custom to whom custom; fear to whom fear; honor to whom honor" (Ro. 13:1-7).

## IN THE BOOK OF 1 CORINTHIANS

### Does Not Have Authority over His Own Body

"Now concerning the things about which you wrote, it is good for a man not to touch a woman. But because of immoralities, let each man have his own wife, and let each woman have her own husband. Let the husband fulfill his duty to his wife, and likewise also the wife to her husband. The wife does not have authority over her own body, but the husband does; and likewise also the husband does not have authority over his own body, but the wife does. Stop depriving one another, except by agreement for a time that you may devote yourselves to prayer, and come together again lest Satan tempt you because of your lack of self-control. But this I say by way of concession, not of command. Yet I wish that all men were even as I myself am. However, each man has his own gift from God, one in this manner, and another in that" (1Co. 7:1-7).

## Being Under No Constraint, but Has Authority

"But if any man thinks that he is acting unbecomingly toward his virgin daughter, if she should be of full age, and if it must be so, let him do what he wishes, he does not sin; let her marry. But he who stands firm in his heart, being under no constraint, but has authority over his own will, and has decided this in his own heart, to keep his own virgin daughter, he will do well. So then both he who gives his own virgin daughter in marriage does well, and he who does not give her in marriage will do better" (1Co. 7:36-38).

## A Symbol of Authority on Her Head

"Now I praise you because you remember me in everything, and hold firmly to the traditions, just as I delivered them to you. But I want you to understand that Christ is the head of every man, and the man is the head of a woman, and God is the head of Christ. Every man who has something on his head while praying or prophesying, disgraces his head. But every woman who has her head uncovered while praying or prophesying, disgraces her head; for she is one and the same with her whose head is shaved. For if a woman does not cover her head, let her also have her hair cut off; but if it is disgraceful for a woman to have her hair cut off or her head shaved, let her cover her head. For a man ought not to have his head covered, since he is the image and glory of God; but the woman is the glory of man. For man does not originate from woman, but woman from man; for indeed man was not created for the woman's sake, but woman for the man's sake. Therefore the woman ought to have a symbol of authority on her head, because of the angels. However, in the Lord, neither is woman independent of man, nor is man independent of woman. For as the woman originates from the man, so also the man has his birth through the woman; and all things originate from God. Judge for yourselves: is it proper for a woman to pray to God with head uncovered? Does not even nature itself teach you that if a man has long hair, it is a dishonor to him, but if a woman has long hair, it is a glory to her? For her hair is given to her for a covering. But if one is inclined to be contentious, we have no other practice, nor have the churches of God" (1Co. 11:2-16).

## He Has Abolished All Rule and All Authority and Power

"But now Christ has been raised from the dead, the first fruits of those who are asleep. For since by a man came death, by a man also came the resurrection of the dead. For as in Adam all die, so also in Christ all shall be made alive. But each in his own order: Christ the first fruits, after that those who are Christ's at His coming, then comes the end, when He delivers up the kingdom to the God and Father, when He has abolished all rule and all authority and power. For He must reign until He has put all His enemies under His feet. The last enemy that will be abolished is death. For HE HAS PUT ALL THINGS IN SUBJECTION UNDER HIS FEET. But when He says, 'All things are put in subjection,' it is evident that He is excepted who put all things in subjection to Him. And when all things are subjected to Him, then the Son Himself also will be subjected to the One who subjected all things to Him, that God may be all in all" (1Co. 15:20-28).

## IN THE BOOK OF 2 CORINTHIANS

### If I Boast Somewhat Further About Our Authority

"You are looking at things as they are outwardly. If anyone is confident in himself that he is Christ's, let him consider this again within himself, that just as he is Christ's, so also are we. For even if I should boast somewhat further about our authority, which the Lord gave for building you up and not for destroying you, I shall not be put to shame, for I do not wish to seem as if I would terrify you by my letters. For they say, 'His letters are weighty and strong, but his personal presence is unimpressive, and his speech contemptible.' Let such a person consider this, that what we are in word by letters when absent, such persons we are also in deed when present" (2Co. 10:7-11).

### In Accordance with the Authority

"Test yourselves to see if you are in the faith; examine yourselves! Or do you not recognize this about yourselves, that Jesus Christ is in you — unless indeed you fail the test? But I trust that you will realize that we ourselves do not fail the test. Now we pray to God that you do no wrong; not that we ourselves may appear approved, but that you may do what is right, even though we should appear unapproved. For we can do nothing against the truth, but only for the truth. For we rejoice when we ourselves are weak but you are strong; this we also pray for, that you be made complete. For this reason I am writing these things while absent, in order that when present I may not use severity, in accordance with the authority which the Lord gave me, for building up and not for tearing down" (2Co. 13:5-10).

## IN THE BOOK OF EPHESIANS

### Far Above All Rule and Authority and Power

"For this reason I too, having heard of the faith in the Lord Jesus which exists among you, and your love for all the saints, do not cease giving thanks for you, while making mention of you in my prayers; that the God of our Lord Jesus Christ, the Father of glory, may give to you a spirit of wisdom and of revelation in the knowledge of Him. I pray that the eyes of your heart may be enlightened, so that you may know what is the hope of His calling, what are the riches of the glory of His inheritance in the saints, and what is the surpassing greatness of His power toward us who believe. These are in accordance with the working of the strength of His might which He brought about in Christ, when He raised Him from the dead, and seated Him at His right hand in the heavenly places, far above all rule and authority and power and dominion, and every name that is named, not only in this age, but also in the one to come. And He put all things in subjection under His feet, and gave Him as head over all things to the church, which is His body, the fullness of Him who fills all in all" (Eph. 1:15-23).

## IN THE BOOK OF COLOSSIANS

### He Is the Head Over All Rule and Authority

"See to it that no one takes you captive through philosophy and empty deception, according to the tradition of men, according to the elementary principles of the world, rather than according to Christ. For in Him all the fullness of Deity dwells in bodily form, and in Him you have been made complete, and He is the head over all rule and authority; and in Him you were also circumcised with a circumcision made without hands, in the removal of the body of the flesh by the circumcision of Christ; having been buried with Him in baptism, in which you were also raised up with Him through faith in the working of God, who raised Him from the dead. And when you were dead in your transgressions and the uncircumcision of your flesh, He made you alive together with Him, having forgiven us all our transgressions, having canceled out the certificate of debt consisting of decrees against us and which was hostile to us; and He has taken it out of the way, having nailed it to the cross. When He had disarmed the rulers and authorities, He made a public display of them, having triumphed over them through Him" (Col. 2:8-15).

*Chapter Four*

# IN THE BOOK OF 1 THESSALONIANS

## We Might Have Asserted Our Authority

"For you yourselves know, brethren, that our coming to you was not in vain, but after we had already suffered and been mistreated in Philippi, as you know, we had the boldness in our God to speak to you the gospel of God amid much opposition. For our exhortation does not come from error or impurity or by way of deceit; but just as we have been approved by God to be entrusted with the gospel, so we speak, not as pleasing men but God, who examines our hearts. For we never came with flattering speech, as you know, nor with a pretext for greed—God is witness—nor did we seek glory from men, either from you or from others, even though as apostles of Christ we might have asserted our authority. But we proved to be gentle among you, as a nursing mother tenderly cares for her own children. Having thus a fond affection for you, we were well-pleased to impart to you not only the gospel of God but also our own lives, because you had become very dear to us" (1Th. 2:1-8).

## By the Authority of the Lord Jesus

"Finally then, brethren, we request and exhort you in the Lord Jesus, that, as you received from us instruction as to how you ought to walk and please God (just as you actually do walk), that you may excel still more. For you know what commandments we gave you by the authority of the Lord Jesus. For this is the will of God, your sanctification; that is, that you abstain from sexual immorality; that each of you know how to possess his own vessel in sanctification and honor, not in lustful passion, like the Gentiles who do not know God; and that no man transgress and defraud his brother in the matter because the Lord is the avenger in all these things, just as we also told you before and solemnly warned you. For God has not called us for the purpose of impurity, but in sanctification. Consequently, he who rejects this is not rejecting man but the God who gives His Holy Spirit to you" (1Th. 4:1-8).

## IN THE BOOK OF 1 TIMOTHY

### For Kings and All Who are in Authority

"First of all, then, I urge that entreaties and prayers, petitions and thanksgivings, be made on behalf of all men, for kings and all who are in authority, in order that we may lead a tranquil and quiet life in all godliness and dignity. This is good and acceptable in the sight of God our Savior, who desires all men to be saved and to come to the knowledge of the truth. For there is one God, and one mediator also between God and men, the man Christ Jesus, who gave Himself as a ransom for all, the testimony borne at the proper time. And for this I was appointed a preacher and an apostle (I am telling the truth, I am not lying) as a teacher of the Gentiles in faith and truth" (1Ti. 2:1-7).

## Authority over a Man

"Therefore I want the men in every place to pray, lifting up holy hands, without wrath and dissension.   Likewise, I want women to adorn themselves with proper clothing, modestly and discreetly, not with braided hair and gold or pearls or costly garments; but rather by means of good works, as befits women making a claim to godliness. Let a woman quietly receive instruction with entire submissiveness. But I do not allow a woman to teach or exercise authority over a man, but to remain quiet. For it was Adam who was first created, and then Eve. And it was not Adam who was deceived, but the woman being quite deceived, fell into transgression. But women shall be preserved through the bearing of children if they continue in faith and love and sanctity with self-restraint" (1Ti. 2:8-15).

## IN THE BOOK OF TITUS

### Exhort and Reprove with All Authority

"These things speak and exhort and reprove with all authority. Let no one disregard you" (Tit. 2:15).

## IN THE BOOK OF 1 PETER

### The One in Authority

"Submit yourselves for the Lord's sake to every human institution, whether to a king as the one in authority, or to governors as sent by him for the punishment of evildoers and the praise of those who do right. For such is the will of God that by doing right you may silence the ignorance of foolish men. Act as free men, and do not use your freedom as a covering for evil, but use it as bondslaves of God. Honor all men; love the brotherhood, fear God, honor the king" (1Pe. 2:13-17).

## IN THE BOOK OF 2 PETER

### Who Indulge the Flesh in its Corrupt Desires and Despise Authority

"For if God did not spare angels when they sinned, but cast them into hell and committed them to pits of darkness, reserved for judgment; and did not spare the ancient world, but preserved Noah, a preacher of righteousness, with seven others, when He brought a flood upon the world of the ungodly; and if He condemned the cities of Sodom and Gomorrah to destruction by reducing them to ashes, having made them an example to those who would live ungodly thereafter; and if He rescued righteous Lot, oppressed by the sensual conduct of unprincipled men (for by what he saw and heard that righteous man, while living among them, felt his righteous soul tormented day after day with their lawless deeds), then the Lord knows how to rescue the godly from temptation, and to keep the unrighteous under punishment for the day of judgment, and especially those who indulge the flesh in its corrupt desires and despise authority. Daring, self-willed, they do not tremble when they revile angelic majesties,  whereas angels who are greater in might and power do not bring a reviling judgment against them before the Lord.  But these, like unreasoning animals, born as creatures of instinct to be captured and killed, reviling where they have no knowledge, will in the destruction of those creatures also be destroyed, suffering wrong as the wages of doing wrong. They count it a pleasure to revel in the daytime. They are stains and blemishes, reveling in their deceptions, as they carouse with you, having eyes full of adultery and that never cease from sin, enticing unstable souls, having a heart trained in greed, accursed children; forsaking the right way they have gone astray, having followed the way of Balaam, the son of Beor, who loved the wages of unrighteousness, but he received a rebuke for his own transgression; for a dumb donkey, speaking with a voice of a man, restrained the madness of the prophet" (2Pe. 2:4-16).

## IN THE BOOK OF JUDE

## Reject Authority, and Revile Angelic Majesties

"Yet in the same manner these men, also by dreaming, defile the flesh, and reject authority, and revile angelic majesties. But Michael the archangel, when he disputed with the devil and argued about the body of Moses, did not dare pronounce against him a railing judgment, but said, 'The Lord rebuke you.' But these men revile the things which they do not understand; and the things which they know by instinct, like unreasoning animals, by these things they are destroyed. Woe to them! For they have gone the way of Cain, and for pay they have rushed headlong into the error of Balaam, and perished in the rebellion of Korah. These men are those who are hidden reefs in your love feasts when they feast with you without fear, caring for themselves; clouds without water, carried along by winds; autumn trees without fruit, doubly dead, uprooted; wild waves of the sea, casting up their own shame like foam; wandering stars, for whom the black darkness has been reserved forever" (Jude 1:8-13).

## Our Lord, be Glory, Majesty, Dominion and Authority

"Now to Him who is able to keep you from stumbling, and to make you stand in the presence of His glory blameless with great joy, to the only God our Savior, through Jesus Christ our Lord, be glory, majesty, dominion and authority, before all time and now and forever. Amen" (Jude 1:24-25).

## IN THE BOOK OF REVELATION

### I Also Have Received Authority from My Father

"I know your deeds, and your love and faith and service and perseverance, and that your deeds of late are greater than at first. But I have this against you, that you tolerate the woman Jezebel, who calls herself a prophetess, and she teaches and leads My bond-servants astray, so that they commit acts of immorality and eat things sacrificed to idols. And I gave her time to repent; and she does not want to repent of her immorality. Behold, I will cast her upon a bed of sickness, and those who commit adultery with her into great tribulation, unless they repent of her deeds. And I will kill her children with pestilence; and all the churches will know that I am He who searches the minds and hearts; and I will give to each one of you according to your deeds. But I say to you, the rest who are in Thyatira, who do not hold this teaching, who have not known the deep things of Satan, as they call them—I place no other burden on you. Nevertheless what you have, hold fast until I come. And he who overcomes, and he who keeps My deeds until the end, TO HIM I WILL GIVE AUTHORITY OVER THE NATIONS; AND HE SHALL RULE THEM WITH A ROD OF IRON, AS THE VESSELS OF THE POTTER ARE BROKEN TO PIECES, as I also have received authority from My Father; and I will give him the morning star. He who has an ear, let him hear what the Spirit says to the churches" (Rev. 2:19-29).

## Authority Was Given to Them

"And when He broke the fourth seal, I heard the voice of the fourth living creature saying, 'Come.' And I looked, and behold, an ashen horse; and he who sat on it had the name Death; and Hades was following with him. And authority was given to them over a fourth of the earth, to kill with sword and with famine and with pestilence and by the wild beasts of the earth" (Rev. 6:7-8).

*Chapter Four*

## I Will Grant Authority to My Two Witnesses

"And there was given me a measuring rod like a staff; and someone said, 'Rise and measure the temple of God, and the altar, and those who worship in it. And leave out the court which is outside the temple, and do not measure it, for it has been given to the nations; and they will tread under foot the holy city for forty-two months. And I will grant authority to my two witnesses, and they will prophesy for twelve hundred and sixty days, clothed in sackcloth. These are the two olive trees and the two lampstands that stand before the Lord of the earth. And if anyone desires to harm them, fire proceeds out of their mouth and devours their enemies; and if anyone would desire to harm them, in this manner he must be killed. These have the power to shut up the sky, in order that rain may not fall during the days of their prophesying; and they have power over the waters to turn them into blood, and to smite the earth with every plague, as often as they desire'" (Rev. 11:1-6).

## The Authority of His Christ Have Come

"And there was war in heaven, Michael and his angels waging war with the dragon. And the dragon and his angels waged war, and they were not strong enough, and there was no longer a place found for them in heaven. And the great dragon was thrown down, the serpent of old who is called the devil and Satan, who deceives the whole world; he was thrown down to the earth, and his angels were thrown down with him. And I heard a loud voice in heaven, saying, 'Now the salvation, and the power, and the kingdom of our God and the authority of His Christ have come, for the accuser of our brethren has been thrown down, who accuses them before our God day and night. And they overcame him because of the blood of the Lamb and because of the word of their testimony, and they did not love their life even to death. For this reason, rejoice, O heavens and you who dwell in them. Woe to the earth and the sea, because the devil has come down to you, having great wrath, knowing that he has only a short time'" (Rev. 12:7-12).

## His Throne and Great Authority

"And he stood on the sand of the seashore. And I saw a beast coming up out of the sea, having ten horns and seven heads, and on his horns were ten diadems, and on his heads were blasphemous names. And the beast which I saw was like a leopard, and his feet were like those of a bear, and his mouth like the mouth of a lion. And the dragon gave him his power and his throne and great authority. And I saw one of his heads as if it had been slain, and his fatal wound was healed. And the whole earth was amazed and followed after the beast; and they worshiped the dragon, because he gave his authority to the beast; and they worshiped the beast, saying, 'Who is like the beast, and who is able to wage war with him?' And there was given to him a mouth speaking arrogant words and blasphemies; and authority to act for forty-two months was given to him. And he opened his mouth in blasphemies against God, to blaspheme His name and His tabernacle, that is, those who dwell in heaven" (Rev. 13:1-6).

## Authority Over Every Tribe and People and Tongue and Nation Was Given to Him

"And it was given to him to make war with the saints and to overcome them; and authority over every tribe and people and tongue and nation was given to him. And all who dwell on the earth will worship him, everyone whose name has not been written from the foundation of the world in the book of life of the Lamb who has been slain. If anyone has an ear, let him hear. If anyone is destined for captivity, to captivity he goes; if anyone kills with the sword, with the sword he must be killed. Here is the perseverance and the faith of the saints" (Rev. 13:7-10).

## He Exercises All the Authority

"And I saw another beast coming up out of the earth; and he had two horns like a lamb, and he spoke as a dragon. And he exercises all the authority of the first beast in his presence. And he makes the earth and those who dwell in it to worship the first beast, whose fatal wound was healed. And he performs great signs, so that he even makes fire come down out of heaven to the earth in the presence of men. And he deceives those who dwell on the earth because of the signs which it was given him to perform in the presence of the beast, telling those who dwell on the earth to make an image to the beast who "had the wound of the sword and has come to life. And there was given to him to give breath to the image of the beast, that the image of the beast might even speak and cause as many as do not worship the image of the beast to be killed. And he causes all, the small and the great, and the rich and the poor, and the free men and the slaves, to be given a mark on their right hand, or on their forehead, and he provides that no one should be able to buy or to sell, except the one who has the mark, either the name of the beast or the number of his name. Here is wisdom. Let him who has understanding calculate the number of the beast, for the number is that of a man; and his number is six hundred and sixty-six" (Rev. 13:11-18).

## They Receive Authority as Kings

"The beast that you saw was and is not, and is about to come up out of the abyss and to go to destruction. And those who dwell on the earth will wonder, whose name has not been written in the book of life from the foundation of the world, when they see the beast, that he was and is not and will come. Here is the mind which has wisdom. The seven heads are seven mountains on which the woman sits, and they are seven kings; five have fallen, one is, the other has not yet come; and when he comes, he must remain a little while. And the beast which was and is not, is himself also an eighth, and is one of the seven, and he goes to destruction. And the ten horns which you saw are ten kings, who have not yet received a kingdom, but they receive authority as kings with the beast for one hour. These have one purpose and they give their power and authority to the beast. These will wage war against the Lamb, and the Lamb will overcome them, because He is Lord of lords and King of kings, and those who are with Him are the called and chosen and faithful" (Rev. 17:8-14).

## Having Great Authority

"After these things I saw another angel coming down from heaven, having great authority, and the earth was illumined with his glory. And he cried out with a mighty voice, saying, 'Fallen, fallen is Babylon the great! And she has become a dwelling place of demons and a prison of every unclean spirit, and a prison of every unclean and hateful bird. For all the nations have drunk of the wine of the passion of her immorality, and the kings of the earth have committed acts of immorality with her, and the merchants of the earth have become rich by the wealth of her sensuality'" (Rev. 18:1-3).

# DAILY FAITH CONFESSIONS

(These are not direct quotations from the Bible but are paraphrased confessions based on scripture.)
**SAY THEM OUT LOUD.**

I am God's child (Jn. 1:12). I am royalty (1 Pet. 2:9). I am hidden with Christ in God (Col. 3:3). I am united with the Lord (1 Cor. 6:17). I am a friend of Christ (Jn. 15:15). I am raised up with Him, and seated with Him in heavenly places in Christ Jesus (Eph. 2:6). I was bought with a price (1 Cor. 6:19-20). I am blessed when I come in, and blessed shall I be when I go out (Deut. 28:6). I am a personal witness of Christ (Acts 1:8). I am a saint who prays in the Holy Spirit to keep myself in the love of God (Jude 1:20-21). I draw near with confidence to the throne of grace (Heb. 4:16). I have been adopted by the Father (Eph. 1:5). I am the salt and light of the earth (Mt. 5:13). I am the head and not the tail, and I am above, and not underneath. I am the lender and not the borrower (Deut. 28:13). I have authority to trample serpents and scorpions and over all the power of the enemy (Lk. 10:19). I am a member of the body of Christ (1 Cor. 12:27). God blessed me to be fruitful, and multiply, and replenish the earth, and subdue it: and have dominion (Gen. 1:28). I cannot be separated from God's love (Ro. 8:39). The good work God has begun in me will be perfected (Phil. 1:5). I can do all things through Christ who strengthens me (Phil. 4:13). No weapon that is formed against me will prosper (Is. 54:17). So then faith cometh by hearing, and hearing by the word of God (Ro. 10:17 KJV). Faith is my currency to operate in the kingdom of God (Ro. 14:23). I am God's workmanship created in Christ Jesus for good works, which God prepared beforehand (Eph. 2:10). I have been appointed to bear fruit, and that my fruit would remain (Jn. 15:16). I am being wise when I am winning souls for King Jesus (Pr. 11:30). My body is the temple of the Holy Spirit (1 Cor. 6:19). I have access to God through the Holy Spirit (Eph. 2:18). I have been justified (Ro. 5:1). Therefore there is now no condemnation for those who are in Christ Jesus (Ro. 8:1). Greater is He who is in me than he who is in the world (1 Jn. 4:4). I will do greater works than Jesus because He went to the Father (Jn. 14:12). As God was with Moses, He will be with me; God will not fail me or forsake me (Jos. 1:5). I see myself the way God see me. God sees me as a king (Gen, 17:6, Rev. 1:6) God sees me as royalty (1 Pet. 2:9). God sees me as the righteousness of God in Christ, bold as a lion (Ro. 3:22, Pr. 28:1). God sees me without spot or wrinkle because of the blood of Jesus (1 Pet. 1:19). I am having faith for big things because God owns everything and I'm His son (Ps. 24:1). No man will be able to stand before me all the days of my life (Jos. 1:5). My Father is glorified by this that I bear much fruit, and proves I'm a disciple (see Jn. 15:8). I think big and confess big things because God is big (Ps. 24:1). I will respect God for the big God that He is and my mouth will create whatever I want (Lk. 6:45). I no longer think of millions, my renewed mind thinks of billions because the wealth of the wicked is laid up for the righteous (Pr. 13:22). The sinner's job is to gather and collect for the one who is good in God's sight (Ecc. 2:26). Redemption is not complete without prosperity. Jesus hung on the cross so I can have the whole package, not just salvation (2 Cor. 8:9). I don't have to qualify, Jesus has qualified me. Jesus reversed the curse. The devil is a liar, and Jesus is the Messiah. Jesus is made unto me wisdom, righteousness, sanctification, and redemption (1 Cor. 1:30). I submit to God, I resist the devil and he flees from me (Jas. 4:7). For God has not given me the spirit of fear; but of power, and of love, and of a sound mind (2 Tim. 1:7). The Holy Spirit will teach me all things (Jn. 14:26). The Holy Spirit will guide me into all truth (Jn.16:13). The Holy Spirit abides in me, and I don't need anyone to teach me, but the anointing teaches me all things (1 Jn. 2:27). I quench fiery darts from the wicked one with the shield of faith (Eph. 6:16). I stand firm against the schemes of the devil (Eph. 6:11). I already have the victory and Satan cannot back me up. I advance and hold. Advance and hold to victory after victory (2 Cor. 2:14). I walk in love and live by faith (Gal. 5:6). I have been redeemed from the curse of the law, poverty, sickness, and spiritual death (Gal. 3:13; Deut. 28). I bear much fruit. I'm God's workmanship created beforehand for good works (Eph. 2:10). God's favor is on my life (Ps. 3:8). God blesses me and His favor surrounds me as with a shield (Ps. 5:12). The kingdom of God is within me (Lk. 17:21). I have a production plant inside of me that bears fruit to change the world (Gen. 1:28). God gives me power to get wealth to establish His covenant on earth (Deut. 8:18). I am blessed to be a blessing (Gen. 12:2). I have Satan on the run and will make a mockery of him (Jas. 4:7). No man will be able to stand before me all the days of my life (Jos. 1:5). God's angels keep me in all my ways (Ps. 91:11).

# PRAYER FOR SALVATION

**Say the following prayer out loud.**

Heavenly Father, I am a sinner and I need a Savior. I confess Jesus Christ as the Lord of my life. I repent of all my sins. Father, I truly believe you raised Jesus from the dead. I pray this prayer in Jesus' name. Father, I am your child because Jesus is my Lord. I want to receive the fullness of the Holy Spirit. Holy Spirit come into me and fill me so I can be a mighty witness for King Jesus. I pray this prayer in Jesus' name. Amen.

## PRAYER FOR BAPTISM OF THE HOLY SPIRIT

**Say the following prayer out loud.**

Father, I am your child because Jesus is my Lord. Jesus said, "How much more shall your heavenly Father give the Holy Spirit to those who ask Him." I ask you now in the name of Jesus to fill me with the Holy Spirit. Thank you, Father, I received the baptism of the Holy Spirit by faith. I yield my vocal organs and expect to speak in tongues as the Holy Spirit gives me utterance in Jesus name. Father, I plan to pray in the Holy Spirit building myself up on my most holy faith, and keep myself in the love of God, as mentioned in Jude 20 and 21. In Jesus name I decree it. Amen.

# ABOUT THE AUTHOR

Eugene Carvalho is an administrator, Christian author of one hundred forty books, and the founder of Receiving by Faith. God uses him in the offices of pastor, evangelist and prophet. He holds a bachelor's degree in biblical studies and a double minor in pastoral ministry and world missions. He also holds a master's degree in practical theology. Eugene prayed for a translator and God sent his wife Mercedes who has a six-year degree in Spanish from a university in Tampico, Mexico. They have participated in evangelism in the streets of Mexico for many years. They have also traveled to churches all over the United States and the nation of Mexico winning souls and preaching the gospel of the kingdom. Their website for their ministry is: www.receivingbyfaith.org.

# BOOKS BY EUGENE IN ENGLISH

For a <u>complete list</u> of other books by Eugene visit receivingbyfaith.org or amazon.com.

Receiving by Faith
Faith for Every Day: 365 Daily Devotions
Faith Cometh by Hearing, and Hearing by the Word of God
Faith, Hope, and Love
Walk in Love and Live by Faith
Topical Christian Handbook and Scripture Guide
The Gospel Is the Power of God unto Salvation
Seed Time and Harvest Time
Your New Identity in Christ
The Cross and the Blood
The Holy Spirit
The Attributes of God
The Favor of God
The Glory of God
The Grace of God
The Power of God
The Promises of God
The Throne of God
The Holy Spirit Will Guide You into All Truth
The New Testament Church: A Survey from the Book of Ephesians
Vengeance and Recompense
God's Angel's
Prayer and Fasting
God's Mighty Prophets
A Survey of Jesus Through the Epistles

# BOOKS BY EUGENE IN SPANISH

Las Promesas de Dios
Los Salmos de David
Lo Sobrenatural: Lo que la Bíblia Tiene que Decir
Una Mirada Topica Del Libro De Los Salmos
Dios es Amor: Lo que la Biblia Tiene que Decir
La Adquisición de la Sabiduría es Vital: Lo que la
Biblia Tiene que Decir

# NOTES

192

# NOTES

# NOTES